## REVIEWS OF JOHN DALE'S BOOKS

***Dark Angel***

'A vibrant thriller in the guise of a quest for redemption, Dale's novel is incandescent.' – *Time Out*

'Superb evocation of the underbelly of Sydney.' – *Sydney Morning Herald*

'Moral ambiguity and burn-out are givens in Dale's confident Sydney thriller which recalls the world of Jim Thompson.' – *The Guardian* (UK)

'Great energy, dynamic story-telling, intense entertainment.'
– *Kirkus Reviews*

***Huckstepp***

'A brilliantly constructed record of one of Kings Cross's most infamous characters. A great city story.' — *The Australian*

'Dale nails the treachery, corruption and decadence of a part of Sydney society that traces its origins to the Rum Corps.' — *The Age*

'A fine and disciplined piece of writing.' — *HQ*

'A significant, original work that challenges as much as it reveals.'
– *The Australian*

***Wild Life***

'The quality of the writing is seamless ... the strength of this story rests in the fluency of the writing and the forensic tension Dale maintains in his search for answers ... this is an outstanding book.'
– *Sydney Morning Herald*

***Leaving Suzie Pye***

'Brimming with energy and good humour.' – *Sydney Morning Herald*

'Rips along with verve and confidence ... funny, energetic and full of life.' – Helen Garner

***Plenty***

'An authentic voice telling a compelling story for our times. The best coastal-country writing since Peter Temple's *The Broken Shore.*'
– Peter Corris

***Detective Work***

'John Dale has written a crime novel that manages both to enthrall and to break the mould.' – *Sydney Morning Herald*

***Sydney Noir***

'As a snapshot of contemporary Australia, this collection delivers in ways that most middlebrow literary fiction cannot seem to get its head around. Here is a touch but tender vision of multicultural working-class Australia.' – *Australian Book Review*

'Sydney is a good choice for Akashic's first noir anthology set in Australia. The 14 uniformly strong selections feature familiar subgenre figures: gangsters, ethically compromised cops, and people bent on revenge.' – *Publishers Weekly*

'A startling glimpse into the dark heart of Sydney and its sprawling suburbs.' – *Sydney Morning Herald*

# THE BLASPHEMY LAWS

JOHN DALE

ARCADIA

*Il est dangereux d'écrire*



First published 2019 by ARCADIA
*the general books imprint of*
Australian Scholarly Publishing Ltd
7 Lt Lothian St Nth, North Melbourne, Vic 3051
Tel: 03 9329 6963 / Fax: 03 9329 5452
enquiry@scholarly.info / www.scholarly.info

ISBN 978-1-925801-71-2 HB

ISBN 978-1-925801-72-9 PB



*Cover design:* Wayne Saunders

*For Eric & François-Marie*

13 Muharram 1471 Hijri

# 1

Heathrow had changed. Wheeling his cabin bag through the skywalk, he passed multiple prayer rooms and glimpsed the prostrate forms of the faithful. Black and white flags lined terminals ten to twelve. The concourse funnelled disembarking nationals into an express lane and pilgrims into a long snaking line. He stood behind a woman with a baby tied to her chest, her forehead and hair concealed beneath a brightly coloured hijab.

He tried to recall the last time he'd visited the capital. Increasingly he found it difficult to recall key dates in his own life: his marriage, the birth of his daughter. Nothing personal counted. No longer did he have a private existence. Not for years had he celebrated anniversaries or birthdays. There was only one date that mattered.

Forty minutes passed and the growing queue began to shift. He waited for border control to beckon him forward, and then approaching the booth, extended his forged passport. The bearded officer studied his photo under a pale blue light then scrutinized his features: 'Mr Smith?'

From the flicker in the man's eyes he sensed suspicion. He'd borrowed his name from a book he'd read when he was younger; he didn't recall much of the story now, but he sympathized with the character's desire to write down his forbidden thoughts.

The officer carried his documents over to a screened booth and spoke excitedly to a supervisor. The possibility of being refused entry sent a stabbing pain through his chest. Expect to be under constant surveillance, they'd told him. Expect the worst. Sweat leaked into the T-shirt under his bomber jacket and he could smell his own sour body odour. Stay calm. Stick to your story. To fail now would be unthinkable. The officer came over tugging at his beard and said, 'Where are you staying, Mr Smith?'

He named a cheap hostel in Mile End and the officer waved him through. At baggage control the crowd milled around the carousel. Two men in the royal blue uniforms of the SIPs, London's religious police, leaned against a pillar, looking bored while everyone waited anxiously for their luggage. With a whirr, the conveyor belt began to shift. He dragged his case to one side. The lock had been tampered with. No attempt made to hide the crude scratches. Heathrow's baggage handlers were notorious pilferers and who could blame them in these volatile times. His instructions were clear: vacate the airport and its surrounds, travel to your designated accommodation and await instructions. You will be contacted when it is safe. When, how, who—he had no idea. Nor did he want to know details. Too much knowledge was dangerous.

He cleared Customs with a cursory wave from the officials, as if they already knew the contents of his belongings. Then he was on the express train seated in a carriage of businessmen stroking their beards. Reeking of some indefinable cologne, these elderly men in loose cotton tunics, their foreheads marked with the zebiba, ignored his presence after an initial show of surprise that this scruffy kuffar could afford the fare. He emerged from the station wheeling his bag through the tunnel and into the light. It was hotter in London than he'd expected. Extreme temperatures had been recorded across Europe. The desert was on the march.

Handcarts, bicycles and brightly decorated buses choked the streets. He walked along Edgware Road passing men in smocks and sandals, women wearing scarves or wrapped in traditional abayas. The noise of the traffic on Oxford Street was deafening: passengers clung to the rails and roofs of buses, they rode precariously on sooty motor scooters and buzzing mini bikes, they packed into pedicabs and rickshaws; yet even while wheeling his battered bag he walked faster than the gridlocked traffic.

He weaved a path through the shuffling mass of pedestrians and turned down Charing Cross Road past the rows of religious bookshops and stalls advertising instruction in Arabic, Pashtun and Urdu. A blind man was selling shoelaces and razor blades on a street corner; was it his imagination or did the man signal to another stallholder? He was being watched. London had more CCTV cameras than any other city on earth. Under the enhanced terrorism laws the authorities could arrest and detain suspects indefinitely without charge. So why hadn't they picked him up at Heathrow when it was clear he was tagged? Would they wait until he was contacted and then strike? We can take you at any time, was their unspoken message. And we will.

He knew that officially torture remained illegal in the United Kingdom, although dozens of suspected terrorists had hanged themselves in London's notorious Belmarsh prison or bashed their brains out in their cells. Or simply disappeared. Of course, the media labelled all Resistance fighters as extremists with no regard for the sanctity of life, not even their own. Which is why he had not been provided with details of the mission—he could not be trusted with the information.

The terror alert had been lifted to critical in preparation for the anniversary of the Glorious Victory. Three million visitors were expected to flood into the capital. Prime Minister Nawaz was taking no chances. Drones hovered over Hyde Park, Regent's Park and Westminster.

Twenty-five separate police forces, security agencies and paramilitary organisations were on high alert. Hundreds of SIPs were visible outside London's mosques armed with automatic weapons. Citizens were required to notify the authorities of any suspicious behaviour. Public announcements warned on everyone's screens: *There are people among us who wish to do us harm.*

The smell of garlic and ginger made him realize how hungry he was. He ate a bowl of rice and kofta by the riverwalk watching the barges pass under Blackfriars Bridge. Homeless men lay bundled in makeshift shelters, sleeping in bags, others were boiling water along the embankment in paint tins.

The stench of the muddy Thames followed him east. Beggars squatted on the pavement, outcasts from the satellite cities to the north, holding out bowls they had fashioned from scavenged wood and pieces of scrap metal, stockbrokers and financiers, usurists from the old days. He tried to squeeze out some memory of what London had looked like before but he could remember nothing. Up on the public screens, the old King was tending his herb garden, greeting the Grand Mufti, smiling with beneficence at his young bride.

Advertisements flashed across the ticker tape for the forthcoming national holiday: *Get prayer times on your pocket screen.* As a child, he had dreamed of how wonderful things were here in the capital. Growing up in Australia he imagined following in the footsteps of those famous actors and scribblers who had emigrated decades earlier. Now he had arrived for the national celebrations and his blistered feet ached from tramping over the uneven pavements. He wanted to see as much of the city with his own eyes as possible.

He found himself in a noisy, crowded place, which he realized was the Tube station. There were unwashed men milling around the entrance, and women with sores on their faces sheltering inside. He dragged his airport bag between an old man and an old woman who were counting out used cigarette butts from a glass jar. The old man wore a navy suit that was greasy and impregnated with dirt and a bowler hat pushed back from very white hair: he might have been a retired stockbroker except his face was smeared with soot and he stank of alcohol. It was still possible to buy cheap alcohol from the few public houses in London that remained open although the penalties for being intoxicated in public were severe. As he passed, the old man looked up at him as if in recognition and muttered, 'We should never have trusted them.'

It was dangerous to speak like this even here in the underground. Lifting his bag, he hurried down the stairs. Something scuttled across the path in front of him. An enormous brown rat. Squealing, it raced to join a swarm of smaller rats that had discovered a box of discarded chicken bones beneath a bench. Since the dismissal of health inspectors at Smithfield and Billingsgate markets, the city's ancient sewer system and its underground were infested. He could see the enormous rat scratching its scabby ears with a toenail not ten metres away from where two men were kneeling on a patterned rug.

Picked out in elegant carved lettering on the walls of the tube station, it was just possible for him to read the Party's successful electoral slogan: 'Keeping Britain Safe'.

For some time, he stood gazing stupidly at the tube wall, repeating those three words under his breath. What he couldn't comprehend was how the British people had capitulated. How they had watched as entire cities across the Midlands were transformed.

For the ordinary Londoner did it matter now who held the reins of power? For each day was a struggle, especially with thousands of pilgrims streaming across the channel. It was a matter of slogging through any job you could find, fighting for a place on the Tube, praying five times a day, visiting the mosque to hear the local imam preaching about paradise. The Party had developed the perfect system of control for it could promise everything in the next life—and deliver nothing in this one.

He had been waiting for half an hour and no train had arrived, despite a series of announcements in accents he didn't understand. Now lights flashed on the board and an ear-piercing voice promised a train within five minutes but twenty more minutes passed and nothing stirred. Finally, there was a rush of air and a screech of metal which sent the rats scattering and a train arrived so crammed with people that when the doors opened all he could see was a dense wall of arms and legs and elbows and shoulders and heads pointing this way and that. He squirmed his way into a carriage. Soon he was halfway in, but the doors were blocked by his bag and voices were yelling at him to let the train go. He wriggled sideways, and with a violent tug managed to secure his bag between his legs. For a moment, it felt as though he were being squeezed to a pulp between elbows, backpacks and hips, but then he found himself pressed awkwardly against a woman. She was much younger than him, in her early twenties, with creamy English skin. Strands of dark hair were visible underneath the safety scarf she wore as a sign of religious observance.

She was staring in front of her at an image of a malnourished toddler on a faded poster: *Feed a Swedish child today!* Despite the proximity of their bodies, she refused to acknowledge his presence and continued to stare at the poster as if she were memorizing the location where the public could donate canned food and blankets. He was so close that he could smell her skin. When the train jolted she steadied herself by clutching at the vertical rail and the tip of her finger brushed the knuckles of his hand.

He glanced around. If she was alone on this train, it was possible she was a spy. Perhaps she wasn't married although she was at least twenty, and too old to be single. The Party encouraged women to marry early and offered generous tax and housing incentives for women to have at least three children, and preferably five. Ironically it was women and, above all young women, who had in the beginning been the most fervent supporters of the Islamic Party of Great Britain: the promoters of obedience and orthodoxy. They had worked the booths and formed the Women's Interfaith and Friendship Societies. Nowadays you no longer found unaccompanied women riding the tube. Sexual assaults had occurred on the Piccadilly and Central Lines. It was prudent for young women to dress appropriately. Many of them found the Party's modesty clothing, particularly the safety scarf and face veil, empowering. But this young woman gave him the impression of being different.

Once when the train lurched forward she gave him a quick sidelong glance, which seemed to pierce right into him and for a moment filled him with fear. The idea came to him that she might be an agent of the Ministry of Internal Security. Or the IIS—the feared Islamic Intelligence Services. Given her gender, that was unlikely. Still, he continued to feel uneasy, while their bodies remained so close to each other on the train.

The train stopped at Mile End and he elbowed his way through the doors. The lift wasn't working and he hauled his bag up the grimy stairs. He wished he had spoken to that young woman. It had been a long while since he'd known female companionship. At the top of the stairs the crowd pushed and shoved through the broken turnstiles. No officials came out to check tickets. The clock on the wall had stopped at 12.

Out on the street he checked the map on his pocket screen. When he looked up he saw her across the road striding with her head down in her long green and black manteau. She glanced back at the station entrance—at him, he thought—before she disappeared down a side street. Even if she was a spy he was intrigued. He felt drawn to follow her, but he'd hear rumours about devout women who trapped unsuspecting foreign males into adulterous relationships and then blackmailed them by threatening to denounce them to the authorities.

Was it possible she was his contact? She looked too young and surely, she would have alerted him unless she, too, was under surveillance. He had liked something about her from the moment he saw her, but he suspected she was working for the enemy.

# 2

He found the Bed & Breakfast in Mile End, the signs written in Bengali and English. He didn't know why he had been instructed to stay here. Fortunately, he had grown a full fist of a beard. His intention was to settle in and be as inconspicuous as he could. And then wait to be contacted.

The owner, Mr Hoque, was a small round dumpling of a man with two missing teeth and one lazy eyelid that stayed halfway down like a busted blind. His adolescent sons were excellent cricketers, he said, his pride and joy. He introduced Mafid and Saief, who didn't shake his hand. Why are you here? their eyes said. But they weren't aggressive, just curious to learn why this kuffar had chosen their establishment. When they heard he was an Australian they boasted about Pakistan's victory in the Cricket World Cup.

Unfortunately, Mr Hoque said, rubbing his fingers together, the price of his rooms had increased by 25 pounds a night due to the influx of so many pilgrims. 'Peace be upon those who follow the true path!' he said, and handed him a key.

The lift was out of order. He climbed the stairs. On the landing, a poster tacked to the wall showed Prime Minister Nawaz holding up two fingers in a Churchillian salute. His pale face, framed by his trimmed beard and knitted white prayer cap, wore an expression as made of stone.

Behind Nawaz and to his left stood a corpulent man with a thick black beard and a black turban. The Grand Mufti.

He lay on his bed with his shoes on the coverlet and the door shut. The sheets smelled of starch and the ceiling was clotted with the smears of squashed insects. He turned to the wallscreen to watch the news: four male experts were sitting around a studio desk giving their opinions of the election. He knew this format made for tedious television but was cheap and easy to produce. Praise for the IPGB and its stunning electoral victory was unanimous. 'We have entered a post-Christian age,' a German Professor was saying. All the guests were occupied with the same question: Was this the end of the old major parties? In their worst nightmares, the Conservatives and Labour would never have anticipated such catastrophic results at the ballot box.

He tried to turn off the sound but the remote had no mute button and when he tried to switch off the wallscreen, he discovered you couldn't. Instead, he pulled the sheet over his head and listened to the exchange rates: one Islamic Pound was buying 2.5 Saudi riyal and 12 Australian Yuan.

In the distance a muezzin was summoning the faithful to prayer and the wallscreen was interrupted by a flashing public announcement followed by a series of images of men at prayer at mosques across the city. No-one knew how many mosques existed now in greater London, but it was estimated there were over two thousand. He stood up and opened the curtains. His window overlooked a bare paved yard and cobbled street where hundreds of men were kneeling. There was not one female anywhere. Far off someone was broadcasting chants of 'Allahu Akbar' via a loudspeaker. Eddies of wind were whirling plastic bags and torn paper into spirals, and faded posters were plastered on brick walls and fences. The black-bearded face of the Grand Mufti gazed down from the balcony of a corner shop. At the end of the street, another poster revealed in large bold capitals the letters IPGB, which he knew stood for the Islamic Party of Great Britain. A drone skimmed between the high-rises, hovered for an instant like a dragonfly over the tube station, then buzzed away again with a whirring flight. A Ministry for Internal Security's patrol. Now that the government could monitor everyone's electronic messages, the only thing it could not do was access people's thoughts.

He was glad to finally be in London. The mission was all that mattered. He would not shave off his beard until it was completed. The Islamists had taken control of the capital and the provincial cities to the north, and more and more of their supporters were arriving on the shores of Spain, Italy, France, Croatia and Greece and being bussed and ferried north. The majority of native English who had not converted or emigrated had been pushed towards the sea. All along the Party's intention was to replace the host population. Now they no longer needed the minor parties: they no longer needed anyone. He turned back from the window to the wallscreen and saw that the prayers had finished and the face of the Grand Mufti, the spiritual leader of the Party, filled the screen.

He was speaking from a podium in a large medieval hall with vaulted ceilings like a converted abbey. There were hundreds of people listening, uniformed militiamen in khaki, mullahs with their black turbans and Party officials lined up on the right-hand side of the aisle; their veiled wives and obedient children on the left, separated from the men by a metal barrier. Now and then the cameras closed in on a face, showing only the mouth or eyes for dramatic effect. Some in the crowd were brandishing their fists and chanting slogans while a covered woman at the front was screaming her dislike at something. At first he didn't understand what the Grand Mufti was saying although he could see the spellbinding effect his speech was having on his chosen audience. Every time the Grand Mufti spoke the crowd erupted with a roar, which bristled the hair at the back of his's neck. Then he realized what day it was.

It was Hate the Jews day.

'Filthy pigs and apes!' a woman in the audience yelled.

Even though there were no Jews left in London and in the entire United Kingdom only a handful remained in hiding, these were the ones held responsible for crimes against the Party and the hard-working British people.

'All treacheries, all acts of sabotage, all perversions, flow directly from the Jews' deviousness and teaching,' The Grand Mufti was saying.

The intensity of the crowd, the dramatic close-ups of the cameras, the rousing operatic music of the Party's political anthem and the fierce rhetoric of the Grand Mufti began to sway his feelings and he was carried away by the sheer spectacle of this magnificently staged event.

'In the Name of Allah, the Merciful, the Compassionate, you are the best community that was ever raised up for mankind!'

What was so seductive about the Party's message was that it offered a sense of belonging and connection to something bigger than your football team or your home town. It made you feel part of a worldwide community with a shared belief in the oneness of God. Rationally, he knew that the Grand Mufti's words were false, but watching the wallscreen it didn't matter what he thought, all that counted was what he felt. A raw emotion swept through his bloodstream, a desire to be part of a greater humanity rather than a lone individual in a city of tens of millions of others.

Then a face flashed on to the wallscreen. There were hisses and boos from the crowd in the converted abbey. He sat down on the bed. It was HER. The Jewess. The one they feared, the one believed responsible for dozens of indiscriminate terror attacks, car bombings, and planned assassinations at mosques and government buildings across Europe. The photograph showed a short, grey-haired woman with a prominent nose and intelligent steel-grey eyes. It was those piercing eyes behind wire-rimmed glasses that made people uneasy. She was a daunting figure, capable of perfidy and malevolence, an uncontrollable female who was intent on wreaking havoc upon the Party. All that was publicly known about her was that she was a former Shakespearean scholar who had started on the extreme left of the political spectrum and moved to the right after her disillusionment with the left's tactics of supporting the Islamists. Others claimed that her choice of name was merely symbolic.

She had called the Party's leaders 'demented religious fanatics' who were 'impervious to reason' and who 'must be defeated'. Spinsterish, shrill and vindictive, she was everything the Islamists despised and the state media referred to her simply as 'The Jewess', or 'The Great Whore', but he knew that she was Head of the European Resistance—and the person he had travelled halfway across the world to meet.

The voice of the Grand Mufti became a roar of accusations. The Jews were engaged in terrorist activities, the Jews were scheming, treacherous liars, they were the most dangerous enemies of the Party. Whatever was wrong in ordinary people's lives the Jews were in some way responsible. The crowd bellowed and rose to its feet, clapping and stamping bullishly in approval.

Sweat poured down the Grand Mufti's cheeks and he waved a fist in the air revealing a gold Rolex and for an instant his thick black beard changed into a forest of fearless warriors who filled the wallscreen, chanting a rousing nasheed, and marching forward in perfect unity; one of them held up a sword to the sky and in the other hand the freshly severed head of the Jewess.

The crowd yelled with pleasure and the cameras closed in on the tears of joy in one old woman's eyes. People were leaping up and down in their seats. He could no longer hear every word the Grand Mufti was saying over the thunderous applause but he understood he was showering praise on the Party and celebrating its purity and acknowledging the goodness that lay in the heart of the exalted community of the faithful. Then the image of the Grand Mufti faded away, and across the bottom of the wallscreen in bold capitals ran the Party's slogan: 'Keeping Britain Safe'. He lay down again on the bed and stared at some broken potato crisps a previous occupant had dropped under the pine dresser and that were now covered in coils of dust. The noon prayers were over and the Special National Address he had witnessed was to be repeated at 8, 10 and 12 pm tonight on all four BBC channels. How had the world changed so quickly? One minute there were fools in old-style hats and coats with speeded up gaits and horse-drawn carriages and then next minute there were different fools in motorcades. The General Election of '47 was supposed to herald an era of goodwill. The Unity Government had gone to the polls expecting an increased majority, but the election had seen the end of old England. Like the past, Britain was a foreign country now.

All he could do was wait until he was contacted. Above all he must not draw attention to himself. He did not know of what use he would be to the Resistance for he had no specialized military training, no intelligence skills.

So why then had he been chosen?

The wallscreen flickered and resumed its normal broadcast: a panel of scholars discussing the terrorist threat. Prime Minister Nawaz's words rolled across the bottom of the screen: 'Adhering to Islamic values is no longer a choice. It is a duty to those who now live on this island. Only by standing together will we defeat the extremists and Zionists.'

The wallscreen, like every electronic device sold nowadays, was capable of transmitting and receiving simultaneously. Every text, every email, every voice call, every websearch, every keystroke, every facelike and every snapchat was recorded and stored at a secret communications intercept site in North Yorkshire. The Party was all-seeing, all-hearing and all-knowing. Any sound that he made, above the level of a low whisper, was recorded, and so long as he remained within range of the wallscreen's orbital eye, he could be seen as well as heard. He had to assume his every movement and indeed his every utterance was being recorded, even when he slept.

In Australia, he had learned to live a double life. If you didn't agree with the orthodoxies and opinions expressed in the workplace and on social media then you could find yourself ostracized or de-friended. For your own survival, you needed to conform. He had managed to do this by confining himself to agreeing with those people and causes that were deemed worthy. Nobody knew his real thoughts. At university, his lecturers had suspected that his political orthodoxy was not perfect. Orthodoxy meant parroting the ideas that were handed down. He'd learned to censor his every word and action. And yet somehow the movement had known.

It began with a rally in Sydney in opposition to the 'diversification' of St Stephens church in Newtown. *Diversification* was the new word for the conversion of non-Muslim places of worship. He had been too timid to join the rally but had watched from a distance as riot police dispersed protestors with pepper spray, and there was a moment in which the expression in his eyes might conceivably have betrayed him. For he had exchanged glances with a burly working-class fellow with a coarse red face and broken nose like a former rugby player. There was a second when he knew—that this man with the busted-up face was thinking the same thing as himself. 'We are on the same side here and there are others who feel exactly like you do,' the man's eyes seemed to say to him, 'but we are fighting back.'

And then the moment was gone, and the man with the capillaried face vanished into the crowd. He searched for him in the side streets, convinced finally he had found someone he could trust. What it did was to keep alive in him the belief that others besides himself were the sworn enemies of the Islamists. It was a war undeclared, but a war nonetheless. He knew about the vast underground networks that existed across France, Denmark, the Netherlands, Austria and Germany, the assassinations and bombings allegedly carried out by the European Resistance Army.

The idea of following up on his momentary contact with that burly working fellow crossed his mind. But how would he find him? He had to wait and watch, stay alert, ready to be activated in case they made contact. Even in the loneliness in which he lived the one thought that gave him solace was that at some point in the future he was destined to make an impact on this world.

A knock at the door disturbed his thoughts. He got up from the bed and answered it. A woman with her hair in a grey scarf stood there holding a dirty toothbrush and a spray can of Exit Mould.

'I'm Mrs Hoque,' she said, trying to peer behind him. 'I wanted to know if everything is alright with your room.'

He wanted to mention the crushed potato crisps under the dresser but that would mean her coming in and nosing around so he said, 'Thank you, Mrs Hoque, everything is perfect.' Unlike her husband, she was Albanian or perhaps Bulgarian, and either a spy or a sticky beak. Most likely the latter.

'Anything I can do to make your stay a pleasant one, Mr Smith... We don't get many Australians coming here. S'pose you'd be used to this terrible heat?'

The way she glanced behind him made him suspicious.

'Sing out if you need anything,' she said, casting her eyes over his luggage. 'We can hire you a bicycle or book you on a sightseeing tour—'

'That's very kind of you, Mrs Hoque.'

'I'm a convert myself. Did you watch the speech? Don't spare a single one of them is what I say. What do you think, Mr Smith?'

'Oh yes, I agree completely,' he said. He closed the door. He could hear her scrubbing the skirting boards in the corridor while humming the Party's anthem. The smell of mould killer seeped under his door. It was understandable why Mrs Hoque was sniffing around. It was incumbent on loyal citizens like her to report suspicious comings and goings. When planning an attack, saboteurs and right-wing extremists always preferred rental accommodation, and used fake passports. That is why the wallscreens, and pocketscreens which everyone carried, were left permanently on.

Good citizens were never alone and families who did not watch their set hours of state propaganda every night were viewed as suspicious. The Party's intention was to fill every spare moment with thoughts of the afterlife. He found it hard to believe that thirty-three years ago, when he was born, it was a different world. And yet some things remained the same. A familiar noise from the street drew him to the window. Two veiled women draped from head to toe like expensively-wrapped gifts appeared on the balcony opposite but when they spotted him standing at his window they retreated indoors, giggling. Down in the alley below the Hoque boys were playing cricket with a bunch of older boys using garbage bins for wickets. They wore green bandanas which indicated they belonged to one of the Youth Militias. The Party had set up dozens of propaganda and pressure groups catering for the under 21s. There was even a Hijabi Righteous Brigade, named after a seventh century poetess. All the untamed energy of youth, which had previously been wasted on partying, drugs, pop music, and cheap alcohol, was now channelled outwards against blasphemers, disbelievers and sinfulness. Who would have imagined that British children as young as nine and ten would become so indoctrinated that they were the most impassioned followers of the government and the eyes and ears of the Party.

Not for the first time he asked himself why the Resistance had selected this place to accommodate him. What did they expect him to achieve in this crummy B&B? There were too many Islamists in London, let alone Europe, to kill them all. All you could do was kill the fundamental Islamist belief that men and women were not equal.

Yet he clung to the slim hope that this mission might make a difference. The past was dying; the future was frightening. Despondency descended over him. He needed to clear his mind of the oppressive confines of his room. He took a newly minted pound out of his pocket. There, too, in clear tiny lettering, the slogan *Islam is Peace* was inscribed, and on the other side of the coin the head of the young King before his conversion and re-marriage. He flipped the coin. Heads he would go out, tails stay in. The young King stared up at him from the floor.

He stopped again at the poster of Nawaz on the landing. At the end of the hallway Mrs Hoque left off her scrubbing and nodded at him approvingly. The Party had appropriated Churchill for their own aims, reworked his words and imitated his disdain for critics. They sold themselves as the authentic heirs to Britain's greatest war-time leader, the only political party capable of protecting the true believers, of opposing the Zionists and reactionaries who would do us harm, the only party capable of keeping Britain safe. It was far easier than people imagined to reach into the dung heap of history and pull out some distorted fact to bolster your deeds. The Party claimed that Churchill had been a secret sympathiser for the Islamist cause, that he had declared the establishment of a Palestinian state 'a tremendous event'.

He knew that Churchill had been involved with the Balfour Declaration, but where exactly did this knowledge exist? If he checked Wikipedia, it would confirm that the Party was correct. It was far easier to rewrite history now that old-fashioned paper books were no longer in circulation. The past was too easily manipulated. You could claim anything. There was never any evidence. Digitised texts were regularly altered and deleted so as not to offend the Party's sensibilities. The Grand Mufti had stated years ago that Muslim sailors had discovered America three centuries before Columbus, and now it was an undisputed fact, taught in all British schools and universities. If you repeated a lie long enough, and if all institutions told the same false tales, then the lie soon passed into history and became truth.

# 3

He stepped out into the streets of East London. A reddish sky pressed down on him and the air was mushroom-coloured. Masked cyclists whizzed by and rickshaw drivers pedalled furiously, eyes darting left and right behind slits in their headgear. Women wearing the jilbab-plus-niqab twin-set, that was fashionable in trendy Knightsbridge, appeared and disappeared like apparitions in doorways. He walked east through Bethnal Green, past sweet sellers and men selling sunglasses, losing himself in the cobbled laneways of narrow houses with peeling doors and corroded letter boxes. Garbage spilled over the cobbles and oily black water dripped from rusted piping. The windscreens on the parked vehicles were coated with pollen and dust. He was somewhere near Whitechapel for he could see Spitalfields Mosque in the distance with its four gleaming minarets. What he couldn't see were any women or girls; there were boys everywhere, playing on the roads, climbing fences, kicking balls, bare-foot and boisterous, the older ones wearing the green headbands with black Arabic lettering of the Youth Militias.

He kept thinking about her, the one from the train. She was a plant; she had to be. From somewhere ahead there came a clamour of raised voices. The Youth Militias had caught a criminal: he heard the man's feeble cries. The street merged into a laneway that passed under a brick archway topped with jagged wire. 'Join the Resistance', was sprayed in faded black paint on the brickwork. Well, he had joined. And here he was in London with limited funds waiting to be of use. Had they forgotten him? Had his handlers been captured or tortured? Would that, too, be his fate in the end?

The laneway widened into a street with an abandoned white goods factory on one side and on the opposite corner a two-storey building, The Cat and Mutton. It was a public house. The first one he had seen that was not boarded up or converted into a prayer centre.

He paused for a moment outside. Do not draw attention to yourself. On an impulse, he pulled open the door and entered a low-ceilinged cavernous room. Men were drinking at dark timber benches, and they eyed him with suspicion. He took a seat at the cave-like bar with its dim light and glanced around at the gnarled working-men from the markets, none of them under sixty. The old man beside him stank of sour milk. Unshaven and in a grubby paisley shirt and horsehair coat, he was staring into the empty glass in front of him.

'How's it going there?' he said. 'Can I buy you a drink?'

'Pot of Marston's,' the old man said to the barman. His straggly white hair had receded at the front and hung long and greasy over his collar.

'Don't have any Marston's, Joe, you know that,' the barman said.

'Pint of London Pride then.'

'We only got what's left.' The barman pointed to a chalked board that listed ales and lagers, all of which, apart from one, had been crossed out.

'Well pour me a bloody stout,' the old man said to the barman and gobbed on the floor. Instead of rebuking him, the barman busied himself washing glasses in a plastic tub.

'I'll have the same,' he said to the barman's back.

The barman filled the glasses with a black creamy substance that smelled of roasted malt.

The old man guzzled half his drink down in one swallow, eyes welling with enjoyment. 'This used to be a crook's pub,' he said. 'Crooks and tarts. They all drank in here.' The old man rolled up his sleeve to show off his inked arm. 'My first wife,' he said, 'she was a tart.'

'And were you a crook?' he asked.

'I ran the barrow outside Goodge Street station. If it grew we flogged it.' He drank greedily.

'What was it like back then?'

'The worst thing now, you never see a woman in a pub. Women used to stream in here every night of the week. Smelled nice too.' The old man looked down at his empty glass.

He signalled to the barman and handed over ten Islamic pounds. His budget for the day was spent.

'Music, drugs, sex, it was all happening.' The old man wiped foam from his whiskers. 'Remember the pill? Came in a little foil packet, with all the days of the week written down.'

He got the feeling the old man's mind was wandering off.

'Everyone was getting a piece of it. You don't remember the other stuff do you, son, but you always remember the sex.'

'So, what's changed?' he said.

'The Tories never liked us having fun,' the old man said, 'just like this mob.'

'You mean the Islamists?' Finally, he had steered the old man onto a topic of interest.

'We didn't have Muslims in those days, well not so as you'd notice, it was Russians everyone was worried about. Now you can't even get a decent pint. Most of the old pubs round here have gone, firebombed in the thirties, lucky no one was killed. This is one of the last licensed pubs in all East London.'

'Do the religious police ever bother you?'

'They get in here from to time,' the old man said, tipping his head back and gulping down the remains of his drink. 'Remember page 3 girls?'

'Not really,' he said.

The old man's eyes brightened. 'One of them used to drink in here, Evie Stokes from Camden Town. She was a page 3 girl … hold on!' The old man stood up and made his way quickly to the urinal.

He watched him swaying from side to side. The old man would be in his eighties. That meant he was born in the nineteen sixties. He may as well have lived under the Romans. The London he knew with its bands and pubs and cockneys and tattooed tarts was gone. So much was changing. The pigeons and tourists in Trafalgar square, the black cabs and red buses, the barges on the river, the men in bowler hats, the inclement weather, the rushing for the tube, the sandwich shops and fruit barrows, the Tescos and Waitroses, the church spires—would any of this endure? Or would it all soon be forgotten, like the tired memories this old man carted around in his toothless head.

'Funny how the past comes flooding back to you.' The old man lowered himself cautiously back onto his stool. 'Remember platform heels, mini-skirts, fish net stockings …?'

A sense of despair took hold of him. The old man's memory was nothing but a meandering path of sexual associations.

'Get us another one, son,' the old man said, 'and I'll tell you about this stripper from Wapping.'

He checked his wallet. He didn't have enough left for another round and he didn't want to hear about the old man's lascivious past. He wanted to know how the Islamists had won control of this country without firing a shot. 'Did you vote for them?' he said suddenly.

'Who?' The old man's eyebrows bristled.

'The IPGB.'

'Me, I never voted for nobody. Waste of time.'

Was this how they'd succeeded—through apathy? He had been told that through the twenties and thirties the Islamists had built up support in the UK, infiltrating sectors of government, the armed forces and police, the political parties and the universities, gaining public sympathy, manipulating the media and implementing their own religious agenda, first at local level, then imposing themselves on councils and regional towns, systematically establishing a parallel legal system.

And yet for the old man, governments came and went, the sky never fell in. Life for ordinary folk continued just the same, people adapted to all kinds of restrictions. 'You get used to it,' the old man said. Besides, he had more pressing concerns: 'The landlady says I smell, well I ain't got time to take a bath every second week, can't afford to neither …'

Soon the old man would be gone and the Cat and Mutton too. He bought him half a stout. The Resistance would not be pleased with him wasting money on non-essentials. He had expected this old man to be seething with resentment, but no, all that seemed to matter to him were the memories of the women he'd shagged and the music he'd listened to and the pleasures he'd wrung out of his time on this earth.

'Remember punk rock?'

'Vaguely,' he said.

'I had plenty of fun in them old days, pulled me a ton of birds, no one can take that away.'

He had never heard women called birds before. He left the old man sitting on his stool and went out into the street, his head spinning from the stout.

Was it better to retreat into your own alcohol-soaked memories like that old man? Life was short and it was not as if he was unafraid. When they caught him, and eventually he knew they would, it would only be a matter of hours before he betrayed his family, his friends, his deepest beliefs. A sense of helplessness took hold of him. He was aware of his own human weakness.

So why had he been chosen? The answers they'd provided in Sydney never satisfied him. They needed someone 'ordinary' they'd said, someone who could pass through immigration undetected, travel under the radar and take a message to HER. He had no intelligence security file, no electronic footprint, no criminal convictions; as far as he knew he was not on any ASIO watch list. Everyone in the Resistance who was willing to undertake the journey was either being closely monitored or had their passports revoked or cancelled. All he had to do was arrive in London safely and await instructions, then his role would be made clear. When he had wanted to know more, his handler, a huge red-haired Irishman with a broken nose, named Padraig O'Connell had asked, 'Do you not want to play your part, son?'

They had let him pick a name for his fake passport and he chose Winston John Smith. They said it was an excellent choice but they didn't explain why. They told him he was a soldier in an undeclared war, that this was a fight for civilization. Politicians, the SIPs and the mullahs were legitimate targets. So too, were any collaborators working in the media. In this war there was no Geneva convention, there was only us and them. He was to avoid contact with the locals. The Islamists had their spies on every high street and in every housing estate. If anyone tries to befriend you be warned …

He realized he had been walking in circles since leaving the Cat and Mutton. A darkened alley led out into the main street, alongside a disused canal where women and children were sleeping in barges on the water and camping outside the gates of a large industrial estate. Hundreds of thousands of immigrants had entered the country since the General Election, jumping on lorries and squeezing into cars and vans and fishing boats crossing from Calais. Lured by the electoral success of the Islamic Party of Great Britain they had arrived expectantly, waiting for the government to provide everything for their needs. And so they squatted in doorways and slept on street corners and begged outside train stations and set up makeshift shelters on concrete ledges along the bends in the river. For their part the Islamists did not discourage them from arriving, nor turn them away. They welcomed the Ummah with fiery speeches and streamers and fireworks, although they were unable to provide any financial benefits or food or even work for such large numbers. What would happen to these new arrivals was left to the will of Allah.

He felt sorry for these emaciated women with their outstretched hands and their large-eyed babies wrapped in rags. Down alley-ways that branched off on either side he passed people sleeping rough. He was not that far now from his hostel, he had a good sense of direction and it was still light, the blood-red sun sitting above the edge of the earth.

What he liked about London was that you could discover hidden buildings in its winding streets. He passed a little shop that sold only umbrellas and another that sold wooden toys on strings. He stopped and stared at a third shop doorway. In gothic lettering over the entrance it read: 'Brays Book Arcade'. The window was draped with plastic sheeting that had desiccated flies stuck in its folds and judging from its exterior this grubby corner shop must have closed down long ago but a sign on the door said: *Open*. It was the first bookshop he had seen since arriving here. Years ago, he knew, there were hundreds of new and second-hand and antiquarian bookshops dotted across London, but now even the large book retailers had gone out of business. Paper was too valuable a resource these days to be wasted on books, and besides, reading was unnecessary. There was only one true text.

His mother had been a voracious reader and passed onto him a love of books, but had it done her any good? She had died shortly before the Great Catastrophe and all the books she had read, all the novels and memoirs, all the reading she had done over a lifetime had been of no assistance in the end. All it did was help her pass the time. He didn't believe reading made you a better person, or gave you empathy, or expanded your horizons, or let you engage more intensely with the world. And yet books were the carriers of ideas. The Islamists wanted one book to rule the world. He didn't realize it until now but this undeclared war was a battle of ideas, of competing narratives.

Out of curiosity he pushed on the door of the shop and went inside: a brass bell gave a cheerful little ring. The interior was crammed from floor to ceiling with paperbacks and hardbacks all jumbled together and many with their spines split and loose pages tumbling out. Books were piled on tables and stacked on shelves and chairs; thousands of them leaned awkwardly against the walls, and lay dumped on the floor covered in dust as if they had fallen off a truck. He picked up a paperback, its pages foxed and eaten by silverfish. It was *The Histories*, a favourite book of his.

'Can I help you?' a voice called.

He turned around and a short, rumpled fellow with olive skin appeared from behind a tower of books. He wore red braces over a coffee-stained shirt and a crooked bow tie. A pair of thick black spectacles contrasted with his completely bald head. He had a long white goatee and the gruff demeanor of an old communist, the kind that used to visit his grandfather's left-wing bookshop in western Sydney.

'We're closed.'

'I'm sorry.' He put down Herodotus. 'The sign said open. This is the first bookshop I've come across—'

'This is the last bookshop in London,' the man said. 'Goldsboro, Hatchards, Waterstones, they're all gone. Foyles is now a multi-story prayer centre.' He pushed past him and flipped the sign over on the door. He stood with both thumbs hooked into his braces peering at him over the top of his glasses. 'You don't find people interested in books these days.'

'Why's that?' he asked. It occurred to him that this bookseller might be a sympathizer or even his contact.

'I owned eleven bookshops in my time. And this is the last,' the man said. Once you start closing bookshops that's the end of it. You might as well pack up civilization and go live in a cave.'

There was a smell of dampness in the air and something worse, raw sewage perhaps, emanating from the rear of the shop.

'Everything's a mess,' the man said. 'I haven't had a moment to sort through things.' He took a watch from his pocket and checked the time as if to demonstrate how busy he was.

Winston saw its hands were stopped at 12. 'Your watch isn't working,' he said.

'It's broken,' the man said. 'I haven't had time to repair it.' He waved an arm. 'Most of these books I've picked up from rubbish bins and builders' skips. People toss them out. It's hard to find books in good condition as all the good ones are recycled for their paper content. I bring them home, I guess I'm a book scavenger.'

Winston stared at him. Was he trying to let him know they were on the same side? Or was he trying to trap him into revealing information about the Resistance? He didn't know who to trust in London and so he remained suspicious of everyone.

An old telephone rang above the shop and Mr Bray climbed the stairs slowly to answer it. He heard floorboards creaking overhead and with every step a shower of fine black dust dropped from the ceiling panels onto the tables and books below. Water had leaked under the window-sill and the skirting boards were furry with mould. There were faded books lying on their backs, with their pages curled up as if they had died, and the dust was so thick he began to sneeze. He picked up a red leather-bound book lying on a table and turned it over in his hands. The leather was soft and clean and an elastic strap held its pages together.

It looked brand new, but when he opened it he realised it was a notebook that showed signs of having been used, but someone had gone to a lot of trouble to erase the writing on every page. He ran a fingertip over the faint impressions left on the ruled pages.

'Extremely rare that is.' The proprietor had come down the stairs quietly and his approach from behind made Winston wary. 'Watermarked cream wove is what it's called. You won't find quality paper like that anywhere else in London.'

'Someone's rubbed the writing out.'

'Pre-loved is what we call that. They don't sell writing paper anymore do they?' Mr Bray said. 'Everything's done electronically now. I found that in an old lady's bedroom, a deceased estate.'

'Did you rub the writing out?'

'No, her grandchildren did I suppose.'

'How much do you want for it?' he asked. Even though he had overspent his budget he had an irrational desire to buy this red leather notebook and record in it his private thoughts. The notebook belonged to a simpler and happier time and these pages had once contained the hopes and fears and desires of another person. The knowledge that it belonged to someone deceased didn't worry him; if anything, the fact that his words would be superimposed over someone else's words made it more desirable. Perhaps in the future someone else would come along and write over his words. All history was a palimpsest, he'd read somewhere, rubbed out again and again and rewritten over and over until no one remembered who or what had gone before.

'Twenty Islamic pounds,' Mr Bray said. 'It's worth twice that for the scarcity of the writing material. Then there's the cost of leather.'

'It's beautifully stitched,' Winston said and counted out his last coins. 'What happened to all the bookshops?' he asked, watching Mr Bray gather up his coins eagerly.

'Can I trust you?' Mr Bray said, lowering his voice to a whisper.

Winston was thinking exactly the same thing: Could he trust this old bookseller?

'I've forgotten the name of who came up with the idea.'

'What idea?'

'Stickers,' Mr Bray said. 'It was a critic from Manchester who recommended that culturally intolerant texts should have government stickers attached to their covers warning readers of blasphemous scenes. Writers and critics are useful idiots,' said Mr Bray. 'It was these stickers that paved the way for the government's blasphemy laws. Lists of prohibited texts were drawn up and circulated to schools and universities and soon only culturally sensitive books were available for study. At first only a few important writers found their work affected, writers like Salman Rushdie. Well, you know what happened there, don't you?'

'No, I don't, sorry,' Winston said. He had never heard of Salman Rushdie.

'My point exactly,' Mr Bray said. 'The effect was that only very bland and extremely dull middle-brow books began to be published, books that didn't offend anyone. Knowledge was no longer valued, only faith.'

'But you still operate?' he said.

'Oh yes, they let me continue, it's good propaganda to have at least one book shop operating in London. The Party can point to it and say that books are still available, but there's no new stock anymore. Even the classics are bowdlerized.'

'Really?' Winston said.

'Have you read Dante's Inferno?' Mr Bray walked over to a small mahogany table and unlocked its drawer with a brass key that he kept on a cord around his neck. 'The Divine Comedy was the first prohibited text because of Dante's depiction of Muhammad in hell. Copies of the Inferno were withdrawn from all British libraries and universities and reprinted in 2035 with those verses excised.' He rummaged around in the drawer.

'Here,' Mr Bray said and pulled out a book wrapped in cloth. 'This translation was published one hundred years ago.' He unwrapped the cloth. 'Hand sewn with illustrations by Gustave Dore.'

'It's beautiful,' Winston said.

'Just possessing this edition could get me sentenced to ten years. I have to be very careful who I show this to.' He let him hold the book in his hands and then he said, 'See the passage I've marked. Read it aloud.'

'Why?' he said.

'You can read, can't you?'

'Of course.'

'Well, read the verses aloud!' Mr Bray's tone had changed and he seemed agitated. He saw no alternative than to accede to the bookseller's wishes.

'Rent from the chin to where one breaketh wind …' he paused. Was this a trap?

'Continue,' Mr Bray said.

'Between Muhammad's legs were hanging down his entrails; his heart was visible, and the dismal sack that maketh excrement of what is eaten. While I was all absorbed in seeing him, he looked at me, and opened with his hands his chest, saying: "See now how I rend me; How mutilated, see, is Muhammad; In front of me doth Ali weeping go, his face split from chin to scalp, and all the others you see here, were sowers of scandal and schism."'

'Stop!' Mr Bray said. He snatched the book from his grasp, and laid it carefully back in the drawer which he locked with his key. He lowered his voice to a whisper: 'If you scoured all the libraries in the United Kingdom and all the authorized websites you would not find canto 28 verses 30–31 anywhere.'

Winston looked around for CCTV cameras. Was this a set-up? Was the bookseller a spy for the Party who had entrapped him into committing a hate crime? But would not that also make Bray an accessory? 'I can't see any security cameras,' he said.

'Oh no, I had them all removed,' the man said. 'People don't steal books anymore. Why would they? The book trade's finished.'

'You don't have a wallscreen?'

'I prefer reading.' The bookseller checked his watch again.

'You should get that timepiece fixed,' Winston told him. The light was fading in the London sky and he wanted to get back to his rented room in case the Resistance made contact. His instructions had been to stay put, not to wander aimlessly around the streets. He placed the leather notebook in the inside pocket of his jacket. Quality paper like this was rare; indeed, it was prohibited to waste it on writing. It was a criminal offence to be in possession of old-fashioned writing material. The bookseller had grown more cheerful and invited him to drop in again. 'Thank you, Mr Bray,' Winston said. 'I will.'

'My name's not Bray, it's Warwick. Isaac Bray died of a heart attack ten years ago. I haven't had time to change that sign.'

He stepped onto the pavement with his heart racing. What if this Warwick fellow was an informer? Isaac Bray sounded Jewish. Had he really suffered a heart attack? Or had he like so many Jews across Europe in the twenties and thirties been forced to flee. He could never return to this arcade again. It was possible he had already compromised his mission. How careless of him to trust in a bookseller. To assume that someone who bought and sold second-hand books could be trusted.

Dusk was closing in around him. The faces of bearded men rushed past. London was so overcrowded it sapped his energy to navigate its congested streets. Strangers dragged their bedding behind them, stall-keepers sold pistachios on street corners and in the distance a pair of black drones buzzed low over Tower Bridge.

He stopped dead in his tracks. Just ahead a woman was remonstrating with the religious police, while a group of hackney cab drivers watched on. It was the girl from the tube, the one with the green and black manteau, except she was not wearing a manteau but long pants and a long sleeve shirt and her scarf had come loose, revealing strands of her long dark hair. He hesitated. He couldn't walk away and yet he couldn't afford to be drawn into her altercation. One of the religious police had her trapped against a café window while the other SIP recorded her name and place of abode in his electronic notebook:

'Your head is uncovered.'

'Do you think that is proper behaviour?'

The girl apologized and pulled her scarf down to conceal her dark hair and re-tied it. Winston could see she was on the verge of tears.

'Are you a registered prostitute?' The policeman asked. 'Your makeup is too heavy.'

The hackney drivers continued to watch from the doorway of the café. Over the awning a sign said, 'Tasty Halal Pizza'.

'Where is your modesty?'

'I'm sorry, sir.' The girl sniffed and wiped her nose on the back of her hand. 'It won't happen again.'

'For your own safety, you need to cover your hair.'

The girl stared at the gutter while the cabbies and Winston observed in silence. He couldn't intervene. If they smelled alcohol on his breath he, too, would be questioned. The woman needed to be humiliated first and then the Religious Police in their smart blue uniforms and military-style boots might let her go. He edged closer to hear their instructions. She had to take her repentance card to the local police station and fill it out. One of the SIPs turned and waved him away with a pistol. 'Move on. Nothing to see here.'

When the police let her go, she took off like a hare down the high street. He followed at a jog. It was reckless, but he wanted to find out if it was merely a coincidence they had crossed paths twice in one day. She bolted down a side street that wound its way along a canal and through a warren of lanes that made up this part of east London. The sky was veined with lights and rows of brick terraces twisted and turned in the shifting shadows. The girl was fifty metres ahead. Up until now he hadn't noticed how skinny she was, she had no buttocks to speak of. She turned to look behind her but tripped, throwing out her hands to break her fall. She landed on the road with a squeal of pain. He stopped. She was inspecting one knee. Flecks of blood were visible through the rip in her pants. She fixed him with a glare as if it were his fault.

He held out a hand towards her, but she shook her head and dabbed at the cut on her knee with a dirty finger. When she picked herself up off the road, he saw her old runners were worn through and her clothes were threadbare. She had pale white skin, large blue eyes and plucked eyebrows which she had pencilled in rather clumsily.

'Why are you following me?' she said.

'I heard you being interrogated back there.'

'So what?'

'I was concerned about you.'

'They like to go on about their modesty, but the real reason they want to control us is they can't control themselves.'

'Are you my contact?' he asked.

'It's not safe to talk here.'

'Can we meet again?' he said.

'St Martin-in-the-Fields. Don't follow me.' She turned and favouring her injured knee, took off in the opposite direction.

He watched her go. CCTV cameras blinked down at him from a building on the corner. He continued to feel a peculiar uneasiness. There was no question that she had fallen over intentionally, that she had deliberately lured him down this dark and deserted alleyway. He needed to behave at every moment with full awareness of the fact that the Islamists had him in their sights. Once he was contacted and had something valuable to impart he would be whisked away in the middle of the night to number 80, Strand, London, the headquarters of the Islamic Intelligent Services, where the clocks showed the time in Mecca. Soon he would be in their sub-basement feeling the pain of interrogation. He would betray everyone. Of that he had no illusions. And this young woman was either working for them or against them.

The front door of the Bed & Breakfast was locked when he returned and rapped on the glass. Some ancient uncle of Mr Hoque's let him in. He went up to his room, sat at the small table by the window ignoring the flickering blue lights of satellite television on the rooftops and took the notebook out of his jacket pocket. What a beautiful object it was, how quaint and technologically simple. Most Londoners had lost the ability to write by hand and with it the neural connections that scientists had recently discovered were most effective in retaining knowledge. On the wallscreen a woman was being sentenced by a Sharia court. It was a popular Saudi-British reality show called *The Justice Hour*. The ties between the two kingdoms were growing closer by the day and many BBC news documentaries were now funded with Saudi oil money.

He tried to block out the woman's wailing and stared at his new purchase with a sense of happiness as if he had discovered some valuable antiquity. He examined the pages and saw all of them had been written on and written over numerous times. When he held a page up against the lamp a few of the rubbed-out words were faintly legible: 'Cold, blowy & overcast. No electricity. Eric very sick, unable to type these last three days …'

The paper was almost translucent from use. He'd have to be careful not to tear it. A pen was no good, even if you could find one. He could not recall the last time he'd seen an ink pen for sale. Pencils were different, carpenters still needed them. He'd anticipated a pencil would come in useful and had packed one in his toiletries bag. He took the thick black stub from underneath his toothpaste and gripping it firmly between thumb and forefinger began to write. Just the feel of graphite on soft paper gave him confidence. For the first time since he'd arrived in London he was doing something worthwhile. It was important to add his words over those words that had gone before. All writing, he knew, was built on the writing that preceded it.

He wrote, 'I despise the Islamists. Theirs is a primitive ideology, disempowering, taking away the freedom to choose, to question, to renounce one's beliefs. It robs men and women of their free will, it imprisons the mind.'

He stared at what he had written. He felt a twinge of panic for expressing his thoughts so forcefully. There could be no criticism of faith in the United Kingdom. Expressing such thoughts aloud was a serious crime, but writing them down on paper was irrefutable proof of guilt. The fear in his gut was mixed with a sense of exhilaration. What secret pleasures a notebook gave. It was like standing on a cliff edge and shouting madly at the sea. His words would not change a thing, and yet the fact of writing down his forbidden thoughts gave him satisfaction.

He wrote, 'Radical Islam is a religion for slaves, fearful, intolerant. I despise its sheer stupidity. What I hate most is that everything is pre-ordained, everyone sub-ordinate to the will of God. If there is hope for Europe,' he wrote, 'it lies in the Resistance. In men and women of courage and intellect.'

He slanted the next page up towards the light: 'Beastly weather. Sea rough, ground sodden, impossible to sow beans … saw a gold-crested wren. Eric still not well enough to go outdoors …'

Soon he would be dead and his words, too, would be erased. In the meantime, he needed to play his part. Like all members of the Resistance, he had pledged his allegiance to HER.

'When the time comes,' O'Connell had said, 'you will know what to do.'

'How shall I know?' he said.

'You will be guided by the light.'

That is what O'Connell had said. It sounded profound at the time but he was unsure afterwards. He wondered why O'Connell always spoke in riddles. 'When you die the light inside you lives on,' O'Connell had said. 'Look for the light within, it will guide you through the darkness.' All Winston's instructions came through O'Connell. It was not his handler's real name. No-one in the Resistance knew anyone else's birth name. Their autonomous cell comprised between 200 and 500 supporters, trained fighters and ideologically motivated mercenaries. O'Connell had fought alongside the Kurds in his twenties. 'We are at war and have been at war for over a thousand years,' O'Connell said. 'We are the light and they are the darkness. Before the Great Catastrophe we were derided and despised, but we have been proven right.'

The Resistance, he'd learned, did not believe in God as a being, only as a spiritual force that linked all living creatures. And yet the Resistance attracted Christians, Hindus, Jews, Buddhists, atheists and many reformist Muslims among its members. Each cell operated independently and acknowledged HER as their leader. She was assisted by the Council of 12, who constituted the Supreme Command of the European Resistance Army. Most of the senior leadership in Australia had been jailed or prevented from leaving the country, their passports cancelled under the Foreign Fighters Bill, but he, as a lowly history teacher, had gone under the radar.

He put down his pencil and read over what he had written: 'The Islamists stifle individuality and truth; they are the enemies of reason.' How dangerous of him to record his thoughts, to leave a trail like this, but he was alone in the world now without his wife and daughter. Although he knew nothing of the mission's objectives, he suspected the Resistance was planning a major attack. Something that would shake Britain from its slumbers.

On the wallscreen soldiers were dragging the woman to the middle of a lot; more soldiers stood idly by a waiting ambulance. The woman had a black stocking thing knotted over her head and she was draped in a coarse sack-like garment. A fat man wearing a white traditional thawb and keffiyeh leaned on a curved sword while two lean Saudi soldiers manouvered the woman into a prostrate position. The woman made a bleating sound as the bulky executioner extended her neck by pulling on the knotted stocking. Raising his sword, he brought it down with a dull hollow thump that cut off the woman's protest mid-scream. He hacked at her exposed neck again as the ambulance moved in front, screening her corpse from view.

Winston closed the notebook and scanned the room for a suitable hiding place. Wherever he hid it, it would most likely be found. He got down on one knee with his back to the wallscreen and slid the notebook under the pine dresser. It was clear that Mrs Hoque or her cleaners were not partial to vacuuming. He scooped up broken crisps, a clump of dry grey hair and coils of black dust and sprinkled them evenly over the notebook. If anyone did find it, he would say it had been left by a previous occupant. There was no evidence to prove he had written anything.

# 4

Winston woke with the word 'Shakespeare' on his lips. It was the code name for HER. Fighters in the Resistance carried the names of writers and poets and philosophers as a reminder they were fighting not just for their own freedoms but for their culture and civilization. The danger he feared was talking in his sleep. There was no way of guarding against it.

He completed his twenty-five push-ups and went down to breakfast. An elderly couple was seated by the entrance. The man kept his nose inches above a steaming bowl from which he was slurping a lumpy brown soup while his veiled wife wearing long black gloves fanned him with her pocket screen.

Mr Hoque greeted him with a smile as he entered the dining room. 'Praise be to Allah!' he said. All the tables were occupied with pilgrims who had arrived for the Victory celebrations, all the women covered.

Families were talking volubly in languages he didn't recognise. 'Praise be to Allah', he replied and found himself a spare table.

The girl serving breakfast was plump and Slavic-looking with piercings in her cheeks. Blue veins ran like tiny rivers beneath her pale skin. When he enquired as to her origin she said she was a New Zealander but she spoke with a thick northern accent. Compared to her, he didn't look too out of place at the breakfast table with his straggly beard and sun-damaged skin. Perhaps that was why they had arranged for him to stay here in Mile End. He pulled his collar up to indicate he did not wish to be disturbed and tucked into a traditional English breakfast of halal sausages and curried eggs. He didn't like to admit it but there were some things about this way of life he was starting to enjoy—like not having to shave daily, or worry about what to wear. It was funny how easily a person could adjust to the new reality.

Mrs Hoque approached his table waving the green rubber gloves that were her badge of authority. 'Oh, Mr Smith!' she said.

He looked up from his eggs.

'You had a caller last evening. A black gentleman.'

'Did he leave a message?'

'He said your tour is booked.'

'Sorry?' He'd heard what Mrs Hoque said, but needed a moment to grasp the information. 'Did he say when exactly?

'He wanted to know when you'd be back. I told your black gentleman we don't keep tabs on our guests. I told him you went out yesterday afternoon alone at five thirty. The gentleman said he'd call by later this morning—'

'Thank you, Mrs Hoque,' he said. He put down his knife and fork. Her rubber gloves were turning him off his breakfast.

'You can always leave instructions at the front desk.'

He looked across at Mr Hoque who was beaming at him from the kitchen doorway. Something was going on but he didn't know what.

'Did you watch the *Justice Hour*, Mr Smith?' Mrs Hoque said. 'Our Saudi cousins know how to deal with these terrorists. Don't you agree?'

Winston turned his head away to avoid her scrutiny. The Slavic-looking girl who claimed to be a New Zealander came over collecting dishes and he took the opportunity to leave the table and hurry up to his room. No-one knew of his whereabouts in London, so it had to be his contact. He'd made a mistake of roaming the East End when he should have stayed here. *Your tour is booked*. Was this code for the mission?

He sat on the edge of the bed with one foot folded underneath his leg. For the first time since his arrival on English soil the magnitude of this mission came home to him. He examined his hands closely in the light, the palms, the knuckles, the raised veins, considering the complex functions that a human hand can perform. Everyone he'd met in the Resistance brought some specialized training in weapons making, technical intelligence, information technology, logistics or social media. But what did he bring? He was a history teacher. What use was a history teacher to anyone? The Party said there was only one history that mattered. There was only one truth. They had won the snap election through a mixture of intimidation and bribery. They had crushed the opposition, but it did not matter. They had to be stopped.

The trouble with the British ruling elite was that they despised their own working class far more than they despised the Islamists. A wealthy sheikh from Mayfair was preferable to a dirty boilermaker from Dagenham. It was money that made the difference. It was money, primarily from Saudi princes and Qatari emirs that had underpinned the Party's stunning success in the northern cities.

He locked his room, went downstairs and waited on the stone steps outside the Bed & Breakfast. The Hoque's establishment was situated midway between Bow Road and Mile End tube stations. In the distance he could make out Tower Hamlets Cemetery where the ancient graves of Londoners had been dug up and the cemetery converted into an Islamic burial site. A market was being set up in the square opposite and older women wearing scarves and long baggy over-garments moved between stalls filling their baskets with flat bread, spinach, eggplants and goat's meat. Families were preparing for the feast. He breathed in the smells and sounds of the bazaar. The pavements were blocked with decorated carts and bikes. For the native people of Britain their time had passed, their influence would linger on, just as it had for the Jutes and Saxons, but Christians now made up less than 15% of the population of central London. People who identified themselves as Muslims in England and Wales numbered 27 million, up from 15.5 million in 2034, and while there were no Jews anywhere, the secretary general of the Muslim Council of Great Britain had said these latest figures showed that Christians were still playing a small but significant part in the diversity of Britain.

A bright red bus rounded the corner, and stopped outside the B&B. The driver kept his engine running and called out, 'Pick up for Mr Smith!' Was this the gentleman Mrs Hoque referred to? The driver wore an orange turban. With a nod of acknowledgement, Winston climbed the steps to the open upper deck and sat at the front left-hand side of the bus. He glanced around him: he was the only passenger. Slowly the bus moved through the packed market crowd.

Traffic laws were largely ignored in this part of London and it was a matter of the driver using his horn repeatedly to warn pedestrians of the dangers of stepping out under the wheels of a double-decker. He felt a childlike pleasure as the bus rolled slowly through the streets and he stared down at balconies and tent-filled rooftops festooned with banners and the Party's black and white flags.

From his vantage point he could see old women in shapeless smocks and bearded men playing with their worry beads but the majority of people patrolling the streets were young men of military age wearing the keffiyeh. At a moment's notice the Party could call upon tens of thousands of these youths to stage a protest or boycott a business or burn an effigy. In the lead-up to the last election it was the seasoned Youth Militias who had fought pitched street battles against Britain First and the EDL and after smashing their right-wing opponents with cudgels, sticks and iron bars, they turned on the anarchists and Antifa. In Bradford, Luton, Leicester, Birmingham and a string of smaller cities all street opposition was crushed. The Militias ensured that immigrants voted as required and older Muslims did not stray from the teachings of the Qur'an and the Hadiths.

The bus drove along Hamlets Way, past the renamed King Faisal cemetery for followers of the Sunni faith and turned up British Street heading towards Mile End. The sun was burning his bald patch and he wished he'd worn a hat. For a moment he forgot about politics and as often happened when journeying through London his thoughts turned to the past.

He loved history. Even at school he could recite all the Kings and Queens of England stretching back to William the Conqueror. And it occurred to him now that he was living in a time as momentous as when the illegitimate Duke of Normandy landed at Pevensey, almost a thousand years ago. Illiterate and unable to speak a word of English, the Duke and his small army of invaders had altered the language and culture of this island to a greater extent than anyone else until now. Despite the disavowals of Prime Minister Nawaz, what the IPGB had achieved in a single year was nothing short of revolutionary. The call to prayer had silenced the bells.

The bus crawled past Stepney Green and the house where Captain Cook once lived. It rounded a corner and pulled up outside a row of well-kept terraces, their window boxes bursting with sweet violets and winter pansies. Was this his destination? He waited. The Sikh driver kept the engine running. A blue door with a brass knocker opened and a man in his forties came out wearing a faded brown suit. He lingered by the railing then climbed on board, spoke to the driver at length about what Winston could not hear and then came upstairs and proffered his hand. The man's grip was firm and Winston saw he was wearing a pair of sneakers with holes in the toes.

'I'm your guide for today, Mr Smith. You may call me Marlon.' He spoke quietly with a public-school accent, took a seat on the right-hand side, and said, almost to himself, 'There is no other life, only this one.'

'There is no other life, only this one,' Winston repeated. And with these few words he assumed that he had finally made contact. The bus crawled along Whitechapel Road. People swarmed in astonishing numbers outside the east London Mosque and from this height he had a clear view of the road as the bus leaned dangerously into a bend. 'Where are we headed?'

'To see the sights of course.'

'So this is a real tour?'

'Indeed, it is.'

'And you're a real tour guide?'

'I'm a registered tourism industry provider, yes.'

'But you don't wear a uniform. And there's no other passengers.'

'Our recent arrivals don't do tourism,' Marlon said. 'Not the old kind anyway. I want to show you something.' He pointed to several boarded-up buildings. 'Around here was a gay and lesbian area and up behind Salmon Lane, a thriving LGBTQ culture: clubs, pubs and bars. All gone.'

'What happened?' Winston said, then realized it was a stupid question.

With a sweep of his hand, Marlon indicated the Royal Armouries off to the left, but Winston was more interested in the guide himself. His jacket was held together with safety pins.

'Where are you from?' he asked staring at his badge: 'Budget Decker Tours'. The way Marlon spoke, enunciating his Ts and Ds, indicated that he was highly educated.

'London,' Marlon said. 'Born and bred.'

'No, I mean your ancestors?'

'Africa. Same as yours,' Marlon replied, taking off his cap and massaging his braids. 'Up ahead you'll see St Pauls. It is not a working cathedral any longer, I don't think the Party have decided yet what to do with it.'

The bus slowed along Cannon street and as they turned the corner he saw hundreds of people camped in the churchyard and gardens, a sea of multi-coloured jackets, windcheaters, prayer caps and headscarves. Men draped in blankets filled the steps and stood bunched together on the flagstones, old women and wild-haired children huddled in sleeping bags and under sheets of cardboard; others had erected makeshift shelters roofed with scavenged blue plastic. Rubbish was piled everywhere. The doors to the cathedral were closed and someone had scrawled their praise for the IPGB in thick black paint over the walls of the south transept.

'All the churches are like this now,' Marlon said, 'providing temporary shelter for the new arrivals.'

'Why not house them in the mosques?' he asked.

'Because the mosques are overflowing,' Marlon said impatiently, as if the answer was obvious. The bus slowed to avoid a gang of North African youths racing across the intersection. Several of them began climbing the columns of Queen Anne's statue. 'Are you a Christian?' Winston asked.

'Not a practising one,' Marlon said. 'There's not many left in London.' An elderly man stepped out in front of the bus and the driver braked so hard Winston banged his knees on the rail. Muttering to himself, the old man waved a hand-printed placard—'Your Government Has Betrayed You'. Dirty matted hair streamed over his face and collar and staring up at the bus he began mouthing offensive comments about desecration and abomination. In the middle of his rant, he was tackled to the ground by two SIPs who kicked, punched, then dragged him by the hem of his tattered coat to a waiting van.

'What will happen to him?' he asked.

'Who knows?' Marlon said with a shrug. 'Stupid fellow.'

It surprised him that Marlon was so accepting of the man's arrest. Perhaps Marlon was right. So many of these old churches had fallen into disrepair and this ragged fellow appeared to be deranged. No-one in the churchyard took any notice of the incident and all that remained now of his presence was a broken placard lying face down in the gutter. The bus accelerated past a stall on the west portico selling sweets, pine nuts and bottled water. He stared at men squatting in doorways and propped against walls, the smell of unwashed bodies drifting in the breeze. Was it too late already? Could anything be done?

Marlon took something shiny and pellet-shaped out of his pocket and chewed. 'How do you find London, Mr Smith?'

'Greatly changed,' he said.

'What's it like in Australia?'

'Everyone complains,' he said, 'but the weather's good.'

Marlon didn't offer him any more information on the landmarks and monuments along Fleet Street, but when the bus turned into Great Russell Street he pointed to the locked gates of the museum and revealed that the Rosetta Stone had been returned to Cairo as a sign of goodwill to the Brotherhood. Other historical artefacts were being de-colonialised or sold off by the Party to raise revenue for building projects.

'People don't want to see ancient statues and sarchophagi anymore,' Marlon said. 'They want to see mosques and modern apartments being built. My customers are not interested in the kuffar's old monuments, they don't want to visit the Tower of London or Tower Bridge. That old Magna Carta history of Kings and Queens is gone, the Party is creating a new history.'

'And what is this new history?' Winston asked. If history had taught him anything it was that when a nation wanted to escape its past, it had to change its past. The bus drove along Torrington Square where Marlon pointed to an ugly nest of grey buildings. 'This is where it all began,' he said, 'University College, London.'

'You were a student?'

'I was an ophthalmologist,' Marlon said.

'And you lost your job?'

'It's a long story, I won't bore you with it.'

Winston stared at passing droves of students segregated in groups by their sex. 'No, I'm interested,' he said, 'what happened?'

Marlon looked over his shoulder as if they could be overheard but there was no one else on the upper deck. His eyes were bloodshot and puffy as if he hadn't slept. He gave a long sigh and said, 'It began in the universities with lecturers who came under pressure from the Party's propaganda groups, then came the cancellation of subjects and courses considered un-Islamic.

'The blasphemy laws gave them control,' Marlon said, lowering his voice. 'Even to question the Party or their cultural practices meant you were deemed a bigot. On top of this, voters from the Bangladeshi, Middle-Eastern and Pakistani communities were instructed that it was their Islamic duty to vote for Nawaz. Millions of immigrants unable to read or write English and recently arrived from the war zones were intimidated outside polling stations by groups of Nawaz supporters. The Grand Mufti called on British Muslims to mobilise their congregations and to vote in the general election to promote Islamist interests.

'And of course,' Marlon said with a shrug, 'the media tried to manipulate public opinion rather than report the news. They did everything they could to keep us ignorant and complacent about the magnitude of the threat. It happened from Land's End to Berwick-upon-Tweed, while in Washington, as you know, they had their own problems ...'

Winston tried not to think of what had occurred there. The Great Catastrophe, they now called it—as if it were an act of God. A wave of despair overtook him and he stared down at the sprawling crowds occupying the streets. He had lost his bearings but he could smell the river nearby. This part of London looked familiar, but it was transformed visually with sweet sellers pulling handcarts and barefoot children playing in the fountains and veiled women with embroidered openings for their eyes.

'Where are we?' he asked.

'Diversity Square,' Marlon said. 'See the lions.' Four bronze statues were draped in green flags with red crescents in a white disc and from the columns of the National Gallery hung a huge banner which read 'Keeping Britain Safe' and underneath in large black letters the initials of the IPGB. The Party had vowed that if elected they would end the spate of truck and van attacks, the subway bombings, and the disproportionately high number of knife crimes that had plagued London for decades. Indeed, since the election there had not been a single jihadi attack in all of Britain.

The bus stopped, blocked by a traffic snarl ahead and Marlon unzipped his purse and checked his pocket screen. His nails were jagged and dirty. He seemed preoccupied with his own private concerns and showed no interest in the old church at the north-east corner of the square.

'Is that St Martin-in-the Fields?' he asked. The idea popped into his head that he might find the girl from the tube. He no longer felt comfortable riding around on this open top bus. 'I think I might get off here,' he said.

'I'm afraid I can't allow that, Mr Smith. My instructions are for all passengers to remain within the vehicle until the tour is complete.'

'Whose instructions?' Winston said. The look in Marlon's eyes worried him. Tens of thousands had lost their jobs when the Islamists gained power and cleaned out the Home Office, the National Health Service, the Ministry of Justice, the Metropolitan Police, and the universities, and rewarded their own followers. Marlon was only one of thousands of professionals who had lost their privileged position. Perhaps that explained his disdain for the old fellow the SIPs had dragged away at St Paul's.

He said, 'Are you my contact?'

'I'm an eye surgeon,' Marlon said. 'I don't condone killing.'

He spotted a spy camera mounted beneath the rail at the rear of the bus. Was it possible Marlon had agreed to assist the Party in return for his reinstatement? 'Who paid for this tour?' he said suddenly.

'It comes with your airline ticket. You're the second Winston Smith I've picked up this year. I'm warning you, for your own safety. Don't get off this bus.'

The bus started to inch forward and Winston stood up. He half-expected Marlon might try to prevent his escape, but all he did was shake his head sadly. Winston ran down the steps two at a time, yelling at the driver to open the back door. He leaped out onto a traffic isle. There was some kind of parade going on in Diversity Square and vehicles were banked up in all directions. He had no idea where the girl from the tube might be so he wandered around the base of the columns and stood on the steps scanning the faces in the crowd. A truck clanked past disgorging garbage in the wind. Of course, they had him under surveillance. He had to assume that everyone he met—the old man in the pub, the bookseller, Marlon, the girl on the tube—was an informer. He could not afford to trust anyone.

He sat at a table in the crypt drinking peppermint tea and watching old people shuffle in and out of the toilets. St Martins was now a multi-faith shelter for London's growing homeless and hundreds of recently arrived immigrants slept in the vaults that had been emptied of human remains. Even though he suspected her motives, he had a desire to see the girl from the tube again. It was not so much a physical attraction as a yearning for female companionship. At the same time, he feared she had lured him here for some ulterior reason. Was she his contact or was she bait?

Just as he was despairing of finding her he felt an arm reach across in front of him and a voice whispered, 'When will you pay me?'

There she was, almost unrecognisable under the dark shawl and abaya. Her face, what he could see of it, was pinched and malnourished.

'When I grow rich,' he said.

'Wait for me outside.' She breathed the words into his ear, then scooping up his cup and saucer clattered them noisily onto her trolley.

'How long?'

'Half an hour. Follow me at a distance but do not approach or speak to me. If anyone enquires you are my brother-in-law. Oh, I'm sorry sir!' Her voice rose in apology to him as a customer passed within earshot of their table. 'Did I spill tea on your jacket?'

'Be more careful next time, girl,' he said loudly and stared into her eyes: they were an intense blue with thick black lashes. Perhaps she wasn't English after all. What did it mean to be called English nowadays? Its culture and values were changing so rapidly that even ordinary English words no longer meant what they once did.

Winston went outside and breathed in the thick polluted London air. The celebrations had begun and Diversity Square was teeming with recent arrivals who had flocked across the channel and now they camped along the banks of the river and crouched in the cobbled streets, hands outstretched for the zakat, weary-eyed from their travels. He had never seen so many beggars before, some covered in weeping sores, others with their feet swollen and bandaged. Two veiled women in black niqabs descended on a teenage girl wearing flesh-coloured stockings and high-heel shoes. Roughly, the women tugged at her scarf, admonishing her for her choice of footwear.

The girl from the tube emerged from the crypt and strode off in a north-easterly direction without a glance in his direction. If he had not been nimble enough he might have lost her in the crowd even though the shapeless black cloak she wore hindered her movements. She was heading north up Charing Cross Road, then without warning she ducked down a side alley and crossed Oxford in the direction of Bloomsbury.

He followed, pushing a path between the surge of people; sleek black German limousines whizzed past bearing the special numberplates that indicated they belonged to the IPGB. Up ahead he could see her moving between the handcarts. She seemed to know these back streets like a cabbie's daughter. Through an iron gate she led him and down a set of algae-covered stone steps. No doubt he would pay a price for his curiosity but she had piqued his interest. She stopped by the servant's entrance to a crumbling three-story Georgian terrace. To the right of the basement door was a converted cellar where previous owners had for centuries stored their coal and firewood. She unlocked a padlock, slid the bolt and gestured him inside. A single iron bed stood under a barred-up window and there was a makeshift dresser, a pair of ill-matching chairs and a packing case on which were laid out personal items including a mirror, a china cup, two lipsticks, a jug of water and an antique turntable.

From what he could see there was no toilet or even a bathtub in her hollowed-out cell. He heard her bolt the iron mesh door behind him and instinctively tried to straighten but banged his head against the low brick arch. She gestured to a chair that had been repaired with different-sized brass screws and ripped off her shawl and abaya and flung the smelly rags onto the floor. 'Thank God. I can breathe again,' she said.

She was skinny with red bites up her legs, and her breasts—what he could see of them—were almost non-existent under her singlet. She perched on the edge of the bed wearing shorts and a dirty top. Her skin was pasty. 'How old are you?' he said.

'Old enough.'

'Why'd you bring me here?

As soon as I saw you on the tube I knew you was against them.'

'The Islamists?'

'Yes,' she said. 'You have to be careful who you pick up, there's informers on every street corner hoping to get on the housing register.'

'Where do you shower?' he said, looking over at the small dirty sink.

'St Martin's. Any more questions?'

'Yes,' he said, 'but I'm too polite to ask.' Her shapely mouth was turned up at the corners and when she spoke he caught a glimpse of her badly decayed teeth. She sat opposite him scratching at her bites, scabies or fleas, and sizing him up as if she was in control of the situation. 'Are you my contact?'

'What do you mean?' she said.

'Oranges and lemons—'

'Says the bells of St Clement's. My grandmother used to sing that, but I don't remember all the verses.'

'Who do you work for?'

'Myself.'

His head was so filled with heightened suspicions that he had not considered the other possibility of why she might be wandering the streets of London on her own. 'Are you a sex worker?' he said.

'I'm a free woman.'

'When will you pay me, I thought that was code.'

'What code?' she said.

From the look of her body she had not eaten a square meal in days and yet she volunteered clearing dishes at St Martin's shelter. Presumably she could eat her fill of their haricot bean stew.

'What's your name?' he asked.

'Chelsea.'

'I'm Winston.'

'You want to hear some music, Winston?'

Since his arrival in London he had not heard any music apart from the nasheeds on Oxford Street. Why listen to silly pop songs when you could be glorifying God? Chelsea placed a small vinyl record on the turntable and lowered the stylus. There was an instant crackle as the needle found its groove and a tinny sound emitted through the single speaker. He made out the words 'You Really Got a Hold on Me', the recording distorted by scratches and popping. Chelsea shut her eyes and a look of childlike pleasure descended over her oval-shaped face. 'What do you think, Winston?' she said. 'Isn't this old music great?'

He read the label on the vinyl. He had not heard of *The Beatles* before, but when the lead vocalist hit a high note he felt an emotional lift to what was otherwise a rather simple song lyrically.

When the record finished, Chelsea asked if he wanted to hear it again; she had a handful of old 45s, as she called them, passed down by her great grandmother and she liked to play them when she felt depressed. Some of her 45s were more than ninety years old and they were her most valued possession. 'Don't get any ideas of nicking 'em,' she said, half-jokingly. As a child she had wanted to be a pop singer and her music teacher said she had a very fine voice. She was twenty-one years old, although Winston suspected she was younger, and she lived free of rent from the master of the house who worked in the civil service. Twice a week as part of a community service order she assisted at St Martin's shelter but she also brought men home when the mood took her, or if she needed a few extra necessities.

'So you are a sex worker?' he said.

'Don't be rude.' Her eyes flashed with indignation. What she did was not prostitution, it was a matter of survival, she only chose men she liked the look of and it wasn't always for money, sometimes she did it for pleasure.

'So, you've been with lots of men?' he asked.

'Lots and lots,' Chelsea said. 'Does that worry you?'

Winston didn't think so, he couldn't say exactly, perhaps it did; she wasn't his girlfriend and she was not overly pretty, but she liked to talk.

She had taken her first lover at thirteen, a Labour backbencher in the Unity government and since then she'd had sex with dozens of older men. Her father was an alcoholic, she never knew her mother and she was brought up by her grandmother who lived in Pudding Hill Lane and who'd taught her that a woman needs to stand on her own feet. She showed him her repentance card the SIPs had given her for 'bad hijab' and said quietly, 'Do you think I look like a slapper?'

'No,' he said. 'I think you look like a nice young woman.'

'I like that,' Chelsea said. Her morals, as she explained, were simple; everything was permissible so long as you don't get caught. She hated the Islamists with a vengeance and said so unashamedly, mocking their stupid beards and their baggy pyjama pants.

'So why aren't you married?' he asked. Nice young English women were not to be found walking the streets of London unaccompanied; they were at home making babies or preparing for marriage. Part of him remained suspicious of her reasons for luring him down here but she didn't seem at all interested in his background or where he came from. Either she knew everything about him already or she had no wish to know. She spoke about her Nan and her Pop who was long dead, drowned in the Irish Sea, while she played him another record. When the song about a sunset and dirty old river was finished, Chelsea carefully wiped the record with a cloth and slipped it into a brown paper sleeve. She stretched her arms, pulled her singlet off over her head and said,

'You want sex now?' The way she said it was as casual as if she were offering him a cup of dandelion tea.

Winston stared at her rib cage and her pale flat belly. Her breasts were small but uplifting and the sight of them cheered him considerably. 'Maybe not right away,' he said. 'I'm happy to talk though.'

'Really?' Her voice went up a notch, possibly with relief. 'Will I leave my top off?'

'That would be lovely, yes,' he said. 'I've forgotten how beautiful the female body is.'

'They want to cover us up with ugly blankets,' Chelsea said. 'So where are you from, Winston?'

'Australia.'

Innocently, she enquired what it was like there. Did they speak English? Was Australia far away? It came as no surprise to Winston that she knew nothing about his country's geography or history. Under the previous Unity government, illiteracy had increased. From pre-school all English and Welsh children were now taught to believe that Islam was the perfect religion and that the Crusades were responsible for the worst genocide in human history. Winston knew it was the Arab armies under Caliph Umar who laid siege to Jerusalem in 637 and occupied Palestine, but it didn't matter. 'There was truth and there were lies,' Sarah had said, 'and if you clung to the truth you were courageous.'

A bell rang outside, a short sharp jangle that made Chelsea jump. She grabbed her abaya and dressed hurriedly, without even bothering to put on her camisole underneath. 'Listen,' she said, leaning forward, 'I have to go. Please don't let anyone see you leave.'

'Who lives in that house?'

'Can you come tomorrow afternoon?'

'I'll try,' he said, but he didn't think he would. It was too dangerous.

'We can have sex next time,' she said. 'Promise me you'll bring something nice. Like flowers or chocolate; I love dark chocolate.' Her smile revealed her decayed little teeth. 'Promise?'

'I promise,' he said. 'What do you do for them?' He indicated the three-story terrace.

'I help out with the children.'

'Like an au pair?'

'Something like that,' she said. 'Did you like my music?'

'Yes,' he said, although he didn't have a strong reaction to it either way. And then the next moment, without warning, she threw her arms around his neck. She pulled him down to her level until their lips were touching and she shut her eyes and kissed him long and hard and he tasted her warm sour breath and felt strands of her hair brush his eyelids and her body press against his. He had no reaction other than surprise. There was nothing fake about what was happening. It was a spontaneous gesture that dispelled all his doubts. She was young and alive and living in the moment and everything she did was completely natural. Then she ran out the door and across the blue path to the main building with its stone facade. He glimpsed a dark red door open and she disappeared inside.

For a while he stood in her cellar reminded of the two women in his life he loved the most, his wife and daughter, and how Chelsea who looked like neither of them brought back memories, not of things they'd said or done—but fleeting moments of intimacy. The Party wanted to kept the sexes apart. Imprisoning women in heavy shrouds with sleeve extenders and synthetic black gloves was done to prevent touching between strangers. Yet touch was such a powerful sense—the one people depended on most.

Winston peered outside then gently pulled the iron mesh door behind him. He took the stairs careful not to be seen from the windows of the main building and turned right into the street past a cobbler repairing sandals, and another man fanning the coals at a kebab brazier. Neither of them saw him, or if they did, Winston didn't notice, and as he increased his pace heading in an easterly direction he recalled the sight of Chelsea's breasts. For the first time since he'd arrived in London he felt alive. No, more than that, he felt human.

# 5

Mrs Hoque was serving a sherbet made of rosewater, sugar and a hint of cinnamon to her guests in celebration of the bravery displayed by her sons. The Youth Militias had captured a thief near the corner store and punished him on the spot; that man would never steal again.

Both Hoque boys wore matching IPGB headbands with jeans and T-shirts on which was printed *Our Prophet Our Honour*. The Party used the Brigades and Youth Militias to cleanse the suburbs of homosexual filth and immoral behaviour.

'It was satisfying to see justice performed quickly,' Mr Hoque was telling his guests. 'God likes to see his laws obeyed.'

Winston saw dried blood on the laces of Mafid's runners. 'This thief,' he asked. 'Did you hurt him badly?'

Mafid laughed at such a question. 'We are not animals,' he said. 'The man was punished by the laws of Allah.'

'And what are they?'

'Justice must be swift and it must be according to the Qur'an.'

Winston forced himself to smile at the wiry adolescent, who was beginning to sprout facial hair. In a year or so Mafid would be too old for the Lion Cubs and would join the SIPs or the Revolutionary Guard. On a personal level he found Mafid to be polite and respectful.

No doubt it would be a different experience if, partially intoxicated, he encountered Mafid and the Militias in an alley late at night.

He thanked Mrs Hoque for the cold drink that was so refreshing in the London heat and went up to his room and lay on his bed. His feet ached from pounding the concrete. As usual the news headlines were concerned with the celebrations for the anniversary of the Glorious Victory and footage of the old King praying at Peckham Mosque. Two hundred and forty dormant churches across England had been 'revitalised' and 'diversified' into active mosques with the blessing of the King and the white-haired Archbishop of Canterbury. Now that the Houses of Windsor and Saud had joined in marriage, the prosperity of both kingdoms was assured.

He got down on one knee with his back to the wallscreen and reached for his notebook underneath the dresser. A terrible fear took possession of him. The notebook had been moved. The thick layer of dust was gone and the notebook was lying on its side against the wall. Someone had moved it, perhaps while vacuuming. He slid the notebook out praying that the cleaner, or whoever it was, had not read inside. His hands trembled as he opened the pages and bile rose at the back of his throat. The consequences were too terrible to contemplate. Writing things down was guaranteed to bring you misery. Now as he read over what he had written he realized how incriminating it was. This was indisputable proof of his criminality. Fortunately, he had written in pencil and if he could rub his words out he might be safe; he could deny them, or blame the bookseller! Who was to say this was his handwriting? When he flicked to the last page he saw a new sentence he did not recognise: 'Floral Street Covent Garden Tomorrow 10 am'.

A sense of disbelief overcame him. Grinding a fist into his forehead, he tried to think who could have written these words. His first thought was that the Intelligence Services were setting a trap. But why not arrest him here? Why go to all the trouble to set up a meeting in Covent

Garden? The other possibility was that this came from the Resistance. They had someone working under the noses of the Hoques. The Slavic girl who served breakfast, who claimed to be a New Zealander, was she a sleeper? There had to be a reason why they had chosen for him to stay here in the heart of East London. He thought again of his wife and daughter.

He picked up his pencil half-heartedly, wondering whether to write something but nothing came to mind. It would have been the Resistance who had arranged his encounter with the bookseller, the red leather notebook left provocatively on the table. Was he so predictable? Winston had fiercely believed in free will but now he realised that perhaps most people didn't act autonomously, they only thought they did.

On the wall screen, a panel of elderly scholars was discussing what designer gown and veil the young Queen should wear to the Victory celebrations. It was rare to see a whiteface on British television nowadays and indeed in most parts of central London. Whitefaces were viewed with suspicion and distrust. Many had been imprisoned for blasphemy or hate-speech and those few who remained had converted for it was extremely difficult to find employment in London otherwise. As soon as you said your name was James or Jeremy they were prejudiced against you.

Not for the first time Winston was grateful for his mixed-race heritage. His maternal great grandmother was a traditional Aboriginal woman who gave birth to his grandfather after a relationship with a Scottish pastoralist in Central Queensland. His skin colour allowed him to pass unnoticed through London's designated red Zones where only the followers of the one true faith were allowed to reside. Tourists, of course, were the exception, as even the Islamists could not afford to turn off the tap of foreign currency. The pound was falling; the IPGB were disastrous economic managers, but fortunately for them it was all the fault of the Jews. Having indigenous blood running through your veins was a distinct advantage and possibly part of the reason the Resistance had chosen him for this mission.

For a month after his encounter with that burly working fellow at the rally in Sydney nothing happened and then one day he was racing for the train when a young woman collided with him on the Town Hall steps and when he returned home that evening he found inside his coat pocket a handwritten note which read: 'Martin Place Tuesday 2 pm'. He took the day off class and strolled purposefully up and down the square, scrutinizing the faces of skate-boarders and office workers over and over until 4 pm, but no one approached him. Two days later another message slipped into his letter box: 'Central Station Friday 5 pm'. Again, he wandered outside the main concourse in the wind wasting his time. When the third message instructed him to be at 'Mrs Macquarie's Point Monday 3 pm' he understood this was a test.

He arrived late to find her sitting on a sandstone rock cut into a bench: a raven-haired woman wearing red lipstick, a red cardigan and matching red shoes. His heart was thumping so hard that he doubted whether he would be able to speak. It had been a rash act to come at all. The first thing she asked him was: 'Are you with us or against us?'

Their numbers, she informed him, were small, the groups met in local scout halls and CWA centres under tight security. An army of Australians who supported free speech, she called them, but if they were an army they were a rag-tag one. Sarah Sobieski was her name and she was their key recruiter, twenty-five, attractive, articulate. Her father, a Polish Jew from Kraców, had been expelled from the University for opposing the boycott of Israeli goods and services. She was more militant than most, her commitment to the cause complete. To be truthful she was the reason Winston had joined. From the outset he enjoyed her company and tried to share her views although he could not, to any extent, match her intensity.

Surely the future was not as bad as she painted, he asked. Surely it'll be different here? But she saw in Europe a foreboding of things to come, and he could not persuade her to live in the days. It was as if, she explained to him one night in bed, she could see the shadow of the sword hanging over their heads, that the West was heading for a colossal calamity and no-one cared to admit it. She was determined to warn others of her vision and she had formed a belief that because of their long history of persecution, the Jews, more than any other race, had developed a sixth sense for impending doom.

It is curious how the dead come back to you in your thoughts, how you cannot escape them in your waking hours, how they swirl around in your dreams, echoing in your memory, imploring you never to forget them.

They were married for seven years and Winston found it hard now to recall much of his life before. From the beginning their bond was intense. They became activists together, soldiers in a shadowy army that stretched from Singapore to Switzerland. Slowly his sense of identity dissolved into hers. That's what love does, Sarah told him: it erases the ego. She had been told after a serious car accident as a teenager that she would never have children, but less than twelve months after they met on that sandstone bench overlooking Sydney Harbour she gave birth to Tess and they took their little miracle to be a sign that they were on the right path. They had found love. What could possibly go wrong?

The sound of sirens wrenched Winston away from his thoughts. He darted to the window and looked down to the street below. Masked men were streaming from black transit vans with semi-automatic weapons drawn. Something crashed downstairs and a voice shouted a warning. A flash of white light lit the windows in the street and a glass panel at the front door of the Bed & Breakfast exploded. Mrs Hoque gave a shriek and an iron voice ordered the guests to remain inside their rooms with their wallscreens on. Winston stepped away from the window.

Fear gripped his entrails. Finally, they had come for him; whoever had discovered his notebook had informed the authorities. He had failed in his mission, he had failed Sarah who would have done a far better job.

He got down on his knees in front of the bed and clasped his hands behind his neck so that they would not shoot him. There was a stampede of boots on the landing and a male voice barked a command. He was sure he heard the words 'Find the Australian'. He shut his eyes and bowed his head in the surrender-don't-kill-me position. One thing he knew to do was confess: don't give them an excuse to smash in your teeth. Then a woman's voice cried out in the corridor. Her cry was stifled by a heavy thud and Winston heard a body being dragged along the carpet outside his door. The sound of boots receded down the stairs. He went to the door and peered over the iron railing into the stair-well. The Slavic-looking girl who'd served him breakfast was being bundled out of the building, her head covered in a hessian bag. She wore a loose nightie that was raked above her knees and she kicked out wildly, sending her slippers flying. From their balaclavas and the Heckler and Koch submachine guns, he knew these masked men were not London's religious police; no, they were the feared IIS.

Winston went back into his room and looked down from his window. Mrs Hoque was wringing her hands at the iron gate, apologizing to the Intelligence Officers for not opening her front door sooner. Glass crunched under boots and two balaclava-clad men hauled the struggling young woman across the narrow road and shoved her into a blue transit van parked on the pavement, its coloured lights bouncing off the downstairs windows of Mr Hoque's two-star Bed & Breakfast.

A sense of relief swept over him that they had taken her and not him, followed quickly by a sense of shame. He knew what awaited her in the basement of number 80 Strand, London. No-one survived that interrogation. Winston had seen the grainy footage. There was no escape. No-one would rescue you, that was the stuff of fiction. If the

Slavic-looking girl was the person who had scrawled that message in his notebook then they would come for him next. But what could he tell them? Shakespeare was a *nom de guerre*. He had no exact knowledge of this planned terror attack. He was in London to deliver a message of allegiance. There was nothing else he could reveal. Of course, his answers would not satisfy them. The Head of the Human Rights Council in Bradford had claimed there was no torture in the United Kingdom but the Resistance knew better. This raid had brought home to him just how dangerous his mission would be.

Winston went down the stairs to a gathering of pyjama-wearing pilgrims in the hallway shaking their heads in awe at the shattered glass and tourist pamphlets strewn across the hall carpet. Mafid was scolding his mother for not opening up sooner and Mrs Hoque wailed and pulled at her headscarf, blaming her own kindness for taking in that worthless girl and providing her with food and shelter. She cast an apprehensive glance towards Winston, and said in a loud voice that although she didn't like to generalize, foreigners could not be trusted. 'I hope this arrest sends a clear message to our government's enemies,' Mr Hoque added.

'What did the girl do?' Winston asked, but nobody knew other than to speculate that she was involved in something serious. 'She was a spy,' Mafid said, looking directly at Winston. 'A treacherous snake.'

Chattering excitedly, the guests trickled back to their rooms and when Winston clicked his door shut behind him he could hear the distinct sound of a drone buzzing the neighbouring tower block and Mrs Hoque proclaiming to her sons how they had harboured a dangerous terrorist under their roof.

He lay on the bed with the notebook balanced on his chest: 'Floral Street Covent Garden Tomorrow 10 am'. It had to be the Slavic girl who had scrawled this message. Only she and Mrs Hoque would have had access to his room. How long would it take before IIS dragged the truth out of her? Rationally, he knew he had to dispose of this notebook but it had become his most cherished possession. It seemed to represent everything he had lost. When you have no-one to confide in, no soul mate or bed friend at night, a notebook is the next best thing. He rubbed the soft pencil over the surface of the rubbed-out pages and teased out the words hidden below. There was a date '12 October 1948'—a hundred years ago—and spidery handwriting he could barely decipher: 'Vile weather, very cold, spread a little dung over the garden … Eric no better today, changed his sputum cup, planted spirea & phloxes ... spotted a number of green plovers and black-backed gulls …'

There was a name, too—April or Avril? And below that another entry dated two days later: 'Eric not well enough to leave bed. Snowdrops all over the place, a few tulips. Dug trench around pig-sty.'

The temptation to write down his own thoughts was irresistible. He wrote underneath her faded words: 'I miss her terribly, I miss the smell of her hair, I miss the warmth of her body in bed, I miss the murmurings she made in her sleep, I miss watching her dress in the cold winter mornings by the balcony window, I miss hearing the sound of her bare feet on the polished wooden stairs.'

He had nothing to lose. That was the reason the Resistance had chosen him. Not because he was a teacher of history. In Australia, his contacts were quiet unassuming men and women who worried about what was happening in Europe. The previous Unity government had embraced the Islamists, promoting the most regressive of theocrats and silencing any opposition. It was done with such ease and so rapidly that no-one had any idea until it had happened. One minute they were celebrating London's first Islamic mayor, then next minute it was the country's first Islamist government. Control of territory, by force or by stealth, lay at the heart of their ambitions. Their radical doctrine was spread in the mosques and enclaves and funded by foreign-paid imams. They lured the host country into lowering its defences while they built up their numbers. Only the Resistance saw through their intentions but even Sarah had not foreseen what would take place in those three American cities. Operation Trojan Horse was only the beginning.

Winston opened the flask of Bundaberg Rum he had bought in the duty free, poured himself a cup and washed down two iodine tablets. He ate the cheese and cracker snack he'd saved from the flight. Somewhere in a brightly lit cell right now that Slavic-looking girl was telling them everything she knew. At worst, she could not betray more than a handful of people. His own role was inconsequential.

He would go to Covent Garden at the appointed time. There was no turning back, for where could he turn back to? His life in Sydney was over. His family was gone.

The wallscreen was broadcasting a speech from London's Central Mosque. The Grand Mufti was scheduled to make a major announcement tomorrow at 1 pm. It was a glorious time to be alive. No one could question the will of Allah for mankind has no will except what has been predestined for him. Images rolled across the wallscreen of teenage soldiers marching through a desert landscape with bayonets and banners waving, accompanied by loud military music.

Just as there had been a Roman Britain, a Saxon Britain and a Norman Britain, now, too, there was an Islamist Britain. They had seized power and would never surrender it willingly. Democracy was only a means to an end. They would change the rules and manipulate the electoral rolls. If they were to be defeated it would need to be by force. Ordinary Britons had long since resigned themselves to the fact that London, with its severe water shortages and critical housing crisis, would never be the same.

Above the incessant blaring of the wallscreen, he could hear the call to prayer outside in the street and the sound of drones patrolling low overhead and the martial music. All this noise was designed to prevent people from thinking. Silence was the enemy. 'A man who thinks alone is sending signals to Satan,' the Grand Mufti had warned. 'Saying our prayers together gives us greater merit.'

If you believed in something even with the whole world against you, did that make you mad?

A forceful knocking added to the commotion and it took him a full minute to realize it came from his door. Hurriedly, he shoved his notebook under the bedclothes and got up in his singlet, jeans and airline compression socks.

Mrs Hoque stood in the corridor, her sons close behind her, their arms crossed. She was not wearing her trademark rubber gloves and her grey hair fell lank and loose to her shoulders. 'I'm sorry to disturb you at such a late hour, Mr Smith, but I want to apologise for that deceitful girl—'

'What did she do?' he said.

'She made vile and offensive comments about the Prophet.'

'Really?' he said. He was shocked to hear it.

'She told me she was a New Zealander and that was a lie. I took her in out of pity, let her serve breakfast, change the linen and clean the rooms for free board and lodging and she betrayed us all. The fault is mine because I was so trusting of foreigners.' The skin on Mrs Hoque's hands was blistered and peeling and she scratched away nervously at the red raw layer underneath.

'My boys will introduce new house rules from tomorrow,' Mrs Hoque said. Her sons nodded behind her. 'We need to stamp out criminal behaviour.'

Winston could hear the anxiety in her voice.

'Thank you for telling me, Mrs Hoque.' He shut the door and lay on the bed trying to block out a BBC documentary on the evils of Zionism. Through the plasterboard wall he heard Mrs Hoque repeating her lines to the Sudanese family next door. Suddenly he began thinking of Sarah again. She would urge him to fight on, to attend the meeting tomorrow.

If only he had her courage. Women like Sarah were the backbone of the Resistance in those early days. Some said she deserved the hate mail and the death threats, that she was a troublemaker, a fomenter of discord and division, but she had taught him that if you are willing to stand up for your own convictions, there is always a cost. Until he met Sarah he did not know that the definition of freedom was the right to say things people don't want to hear.

He pulled the notebook out from under the sheet and rubbed the stub of his pencil over the tissue-thin paper, to reveal what was written. Who was this woman who lived a hundred years earlier? Every notebook entry started with a detailed description of the weather: 'Filthy day, wet and blowy. Sea rough. Finished pruning raspberries. Cemented crack in larder wall & replanted forget-me-nots. Eric sitting up in bed today, struggling with his revisions.'

Whoever she was, she toiled for hours in the garden and planted crops and took the small boat out to catch fish. She cleared a thicket and put up wires for climbing roses and fetched from a village seven miles away what food they could not grow or snare or shoot. She cleaned and cooked and did the ironing and washing by hand and nursed her bed-ridden invalid who spent his days typing up his manuscript. Whoever she was, Winston admired her grit: 'Caught another rat under the house (large brown one). Brought in wild foxgloves.'

He formed a vivid picture of her rising at dawn and working until sunset, hair tied back, bent over in the garden, planting sweet peas and poppies, beetroot and turnips. No wonder the weather was of such prime importance. She was too busy to complain and took delight in the natural world: 'A pair of eagles flew low over the trees at dusk. One of them carried a baby rabbit. More birds around the house, flocks of chaffinches and sparrows, brown owls hooting last night ...'

How different life was a hundred years ago when people still produced their own food. Very little of the English countryside remained today. The Party claimed that in the old days ordinary Britons worked extremely long hours for no pay and were exploited by their capitalist masters. There was widespread discrimination and the most terrible oppression everywhere. The IPGB changed all that. Now there was unlimited freedom for everyone to practice Islam.

He rubbed his pencil across the surface of the indented pages, trying to salvage a few more scraps of information about this unknown Englishwoman's life. All that remained of her existence on earth were these few rescued words in a second-hand notebook. What kind of man was her companion confined to his sick bed? Did the work he was doing survive? He felt a strange connection. He was alone in the world, without his wife and daughter, and so he clung to the past. Clutching the notebook to his chest, he closed his eyes and the last thing he remembered was the Party's slogan rolling across the wallscreen in one continuous loop and a soporific voice repeating the same three words that were broadcast every night while the nation slept: 'Keeping Britain Safe'.

# 6

He woke at six. From the breakfast room came the noise of hammering and drilling. He dressed and went downstairs. Workmen were repairing the damage caused by last night's raid. Given the heightened security threat, the authority's response was completely justified, an elderly pilgrim was telling Mr Hoque. The breakfast room was now closed until further notice. Mr Hoque stood in front of the splintered door frame reciting a special prayer, holding the Holy Book in his right hand, while his second wife distributed vouchers for a nearby curry house owned by his uncle. Winston didn't fancy curried lamb for breakfast but took one of the proffered vouchers anyway.

Towering over their father, Mafid and Saief were affixing notices to a corkboard in the corridor. They were no longer as friendly to Winston; presumably he was now lumped into that general category of whiteface. 'Strictly no alcohol or music on premises', the printed sign said. Below was a list of prayer times beginning at 5 am. Winston knew it was dangerous to stay here much longer. What concerned him was the lack of urgency by his handlers. Why were they taking so long to make contact? Back home he'd been told that Germany, France, Italy, Sweden, Austria, the Netherlands and Belgium were headed for disaster. Perhaps it was too late already? What England needed was a warrior queen, it needed someone to take the fight directly to the Islamists.

It needed HER.

Outside, squads of volunteers and youth militia filled the streets preparing for the celebrations, erecting banners, pasting posters, spraying political slogans on walls and pavements, tying streamers and bunting and black and white flags to balconies and chimney tops. People from all corners of the world had arrived at the capital to rejoice in the first anniversary of the victory of the glorious IPGB. Who would have imagined even a decade ago that the major political parties would be destroyed at the ballot box? Was this not proof of divine will? Was not the IPGB the rightful Party of God?

From Stepney Green to Aldgate, Winston pushed through crowds of Party supporters—bearded men and women gloved and covered. Vendors on street corners sold corn bread, and bunches of tired leafy vegetables he'd never seen before. Others sold spicy flour pastries and potable water. It was a heaving groaning population, many of whom lived off the city's refuse, recycling whatever they could scavenge from the river and the roadside.

Despite their poverty the crowds were giddy with excitement. This was their victory! This was their time! Under the new government the social blights and economic inequities imposed on everyone in Britain by birth and privilege would be lifted. The Party promised to build a bigger and better Britain. London was no longer just for the English: London was for all the Ummah. For centuries, the English had exploited Muslim lands across Asia, the Middle East and Africa; now it was the turn of the English to be exploited. The IPGB spread stories of the waste and sheer extravagance of the kuffar that they had discovered on gaining power, the profligacy, the sexual immorality, the unspeakable degeneracy.

Despite his seven-year marriage to Sarah, Winston knew little about the internal structure of the Resistance, other than it was a network of franchises. The cells retained local freedom of action. He did not know the identities of more than two or three contacts within his own cell.

When he received his instructions, they came from O'Connell. Even if he was arrested and tortured, he would be unable to betray anyone. He was the perfect messenger: disposable if caught, useful if not. Despite his frequent requests over the past few months, the Resistance had provided him with no military training. And yet they had promised him he would play a critical role in this important mission. That was all he needed to know. He was not there to ask questions, they said, he was there to obey orders.

Winston turned up Drury Lane towards Floral Street and paused in a vacant doorway to steal a glance behind him. The SIPs were easy to spot, but most pilgrims wore the loose trousers and tunics, the shalwar kameez that was popular in London's wealthy boroughs. A blind man was selling shoelaces and razor blades outside Covent Garden tube station. Had he seen him somewhere? Winston tried to think. Fortunately, he'd brought the notebook with him; it was too dangerous to leave it back in the hostel. The message did not specify a particular address. He shuffled along Floral Street which was filled with beggars and newly arrived immigrants from the war zones lugging their few belongings, past store windows that advertised chadors and abayas and those long dark coats Winston didn't know the name of, but whose prime function was to conceal the female body.

Gone was Ted Baker, Paul Smith, Agnés B and all the other boutique clothes shops he remembered were here years ago. The exteriors of the old buildings were peeled and faded, the masonry was crumbling, the gutters were cracked and from the drains and vents came the noxious smell of sewer gas. All he had to do was deliver a message of allegiance to HER and then the Resistance would reveal what important role they had planned for him. People with knowledge of the past were highly valued. He stared into faces, searching for a sign, a flicker of recognition. He strode across the flagstones and stood outside the old market, where rows of cheap stalls sold all manner of worthless items.

Winston had a sense he was being watched. He took a step behind a stone pillar and scanned the piazza. It was impossible to tell if anyone was following him, there were too many pilgrims packed into this square. Somewhere a clock struck the hour. He looked up and there she was: an older woman, short and stooped, with every inch of her body concealed apart from her piercing black eyes. She did not speak or make the slightest signal, but her eyes met his and he knew in that instant that she was his contact for the Islamist women never made eye contact with strangers.

She turned abruptly and walked through the market, dragging one foot behind her. He followed her down a stone corridor with a row of open arches on one side, and tall red doors on the eastern side. Brass lanterns lit the ceiling overhead. When she reached the stairs she gripped the iron rail with both hands and started hauling herself awkwardly down the steps.

Men were eating with their fingers at the tables below and the greasy smell of roasting lamb drifted from the kitchens; the men wore untamed beards with the Party's insignia of two crossed swords over the bismillah on their armbands. Winston tried not to stare at an older man wearing a thick black turban: he was the spitting image of the Minister for Culture and Guidance, one of the most powerful ministers in the IPGB government. So many of the Party's elite resembled each other, dying their beards and wearing identical baggy pants and long shirts. His first thought was that this woman had betrayed him. Inwardly he was terrified. He knew his arrest would come soon, knew it like he knew within his bones when it was going to storm.

Waiters squeezed past carrying trays of peppers, field mushrooms and sliced potatoes and platters of sizzling meat. The smell of garlic and steaming animal juices made Winston realize how hungry he was. The men were so consumed by their noisy feasting they paid no attention to him or to this covered woman. Without uttering a word, she led him through a service door at the side of the kitchens and down a passageway to a cellar. There were sacks of flour piled on pallets and in the centre of the wooden floor was a trapdoor covered in dust and discarded packaging. She lifted the ring pull and indicated with a flash of her eyes that he should climb down the ladder into the darkness. There was no light that Winston could see. Either the woman spoke no English or she didn't wish to be overheard, for when he asked where this shaft led to, she held up a palm on which was scrawled in red ink one word: *Go*.

The hole cut in the floor was barely wide enough to fit his hips and reluctantly he placed one foot on the uppermost rung of the iron ladder and then his other foot on the rung below and began to descend. Dampness filled his lungs. Three rungs down he stopped, hoping for further instructions, but when he glanced up the woman slammed the trapdoor shut. There was the heavy clank of a bolt and then silence.

He clung there in total darkness. Panic took hold of him. He was not afraid of falling so much as becoming wedged in this narrow shaft. His shoulders scraped the walls. No-one would ever find him down here; he would die of dehydration in a matter of days. He climbed up to force the wooden trap door open with a thrust of his shoulder but the trap was fastened as tight as a coffin lid. A cobweb brushed his forehead and pieces of dirt dropped into his eyes.

Gripping the rungs with both hands he began to descend again. The musty smell grew stronger and he clamped his mouth shut and breathed through his nose. How far he travelled below street level he had no idea, his thoughts occupied with firmly gripping each rung. His arms ached and his head throbbed from the lack of oxygen. He'd descended another ten rungs when his right foot scrabbled for the rung below and found nothing. He hung there in panic with one foot on and one foot off and—with all the strength draining from his arms—he let go. Down he fell and landed on a stone floor covered with a layer of fine earth and animal bones. A faint light glowed along a subterranean passageway and he picked himself up and walked towards it, bent low under the brick ceiling. Gas lamps were set in niches along the wall fed by copper tubing. It was cool and dark down here with only the soft parchment light of the lamps to light his way. In the distance he heard water running, a stream or a sewer.

He walked towards the sound. Tunnels ran off on either side, and the narrow passageway opened up into a series of chambers. The entrance to the first two chambers had been bricked up but the bricks were now dislodged and wooden coffins once stacked inside the vaults had fallen out into the passageway. Human remains were mixed with the earth and the lids and the broken handles and tarnished coffin plates giving details of the names and ages of the deceased. The smell was awful. Winston entered the third chamber. Stone columns supported the arches and water droplets gleamed on the ceiling. Blocks of stone had been arranged to form benches and there was even a sleeping platform. The floor was swept clean and the air was less noxious. He was staring at the faded murals on the walls when a voice called his name from one of the tunnels. He made out the shape of a masked figure standing in the darkness.

'Are you my contact?' Winston called, but the figure strode off without reply and he followed. Pits and old wells dotted a network of smaller tunnels running in all directions. Some of the tunnels were blocked with rusted iron gates and signs that warned of danger; the entrance to others were reinforced with metal struts. Skulls and femurs were stacked along stone ledges and he caught glimpses of barrel vaults and cobwebbed passages that fell away. Rats scurried past his feet, but he couldn't see their bodies, only hear their distinctive squeals. The gas lamps didn't penetrate far beyond the curves of the twisting tunnel and twice he felt the shudder of an underground train through the walls. Where this tunnel led to he had no idea. The sound of the river grew louder and the gas lamps shone brighter and as the tunnel spiralled downwards it opened up into a cruciform-shaped chamber of considerable size with huge metal doors running off at each end and a domed ceiling resting on four stone pillars. 'What is this place?' he asked. It resembled a church or cathedral that had sunk underground. The shadowy figure stood at the head of a granite table, his face concealed by a military-style balaclava and in one hand he gripped a white cane that emitted tiny beeps. It was a smart stick used by the visually impaired and Winston realized this was the blind man from Covent Garden tube station.

Shifting the stick under his arm the blind man said in a thick accent, 'Do you carry a pocket screen or electronic device?'

'No, I was told not to.'

'Good,' the blind man said. 'Since your arrival you've been under 24-hour surveillance. Everyone you've met, every place you've gone. The one thing in our favour is that the IIS are hopelessly inefficient.'

Winston tried to think of the people he'd spoken to: the old man in the pub, the bookseller, Marlon and Chelsea: was one of them a spy? Were all of them spies?

'The Intelligence Services know your movements. That's why Shakespeare wanted you brought here. Drones and satellites can't track our whereabouts underground.'

'So there is such a person as Shakespeare?' he asked.

'Yes, there is such a person, and she wants to meet you.'

'Now?' Winston said. It was what he'd come for. It was what he wanted.

'She's been waiting.' And with a beep of his cane the blind fellow disappeared through a door at the far end of the chambers.

Winston counted 12 heavy wooden chairs around the stone table. How did they cart this furniture down here? The walls of the chambers were built of old red brick complete with ornate arches. Feeling thirsty he poured himself a glass of water from a decorated jug on the table.

Finally, he was going to come face to face with HER. He knew he was being watched now. His hand trembled as he returned the jug to the table. He had no idea of what to expect. The Islamists called HER a ruthless extremist who dared oppose the Party of God. She was the one they feared. Street posters depicted HER as dangerous and deformed, cunning as a sewer rat.

A door opened at the far end of the chambers and a petite, silvery-haired woman appeared. Winston placed her in her late fifties or early sixties. Her hair was cropped very short to reveal pointy ears and she wore long cylindrical earrings that dangled when she moved and a pair of prominent blue-framed glasses that seemed to eclipse her face. She approached him without speaking and reaching out a malformed hand, loosely shook his fingers.

'May I say how sorry I am for your loss,' she said. 'Your wife was a woman of exemplary courage. I would have liked very much to have met her.'

'Thank you,' he said.

'Please, take a seat.'

Winston sat at the long stone table. The high-backed wooden chairs were designed for elegance rather than comfort. Compared to the other rooms he had glimpsed in passing this one was as cavernous as St Pancras. 'What is this place?' he asked, gazing up at the rib-vaulted roof.

'In all probability,' she said, 'it was a Norman baptistery.'

'But how did it get down here?'

'London is sinking day by day,' she said, 'we eat, drink and sleep over the bones of the dead.' Every word she uttered was accompanied by a slight tremor of her crippled hands.

In a low, expressionless voice, she began asking him questions as though this were an interview for some important position. Perhaps it was. It was a privilege to meet this woman face to face, and he could only conclude that it was a consequence of his wife's loyalty.

'Tell me, Winston,' she said, 'what is the situation in Australia?'

'Bad,' he said. 'But not hopeless like here in Britain. We have to be careful of what we say, but we still retain some basic freedoms.'

'You are fortunate. Here nothing exists except an endless present in which Islam is always right. You are a student of history, I'm told.'

'A history teacher, yes, in a high school.'

'In England history is no more. The Islamists have eliminated history, there was nothing before the Prophet and nothing after him that is of importance. We live in a bubble of ignorance. Children are taught slogans not truth. Muslims are good, Jews are bad, The West is imperialistic, kuffars are racist. There is no alternative view. Western democracy stands at grave risk,' she said. 'So, what message have you brought me, Winston?'

He stood up from the table and addressed her formally. The blind man leaning on his smart stick in a far corner wasn't watching them directly but Winston sensed he was listening.

'I have been sent to deliver a message from the river tribes of Australia,' he said, 'from the great Murray Darling from the Murrumbidgee, the Warrego, the Goulburn, the South Esk, the Derwent and the Flinders and all the other river tribes that have settled our dry southern land—they have sent me here with a personal message for you: We pledge allegiance to the fight against the Islamists, we pledge allegiance to the European Resistance Army and to the Council of 12.'

'You are prepared to do anything within your power to weaken and destroy the Islamic Party of Great Britain?'

'Yes, I am,' he said.

'You are prepared to commit murder in a public place?'

'Yes,' he said.

'Even if it means killing innocent women and children?'

Winston hesitated. He had never before contemplated killing women and children. 'If necessary, yes.'

'Are you prepared to sacrifice your own life?'

'Yes, I am,' he said.

'That's good to know,' she said. 'We have built a great civilisation in Europe and it's up to people like us to preserve it.' She smiled but there was no warmth in her face, no emotion in her voice. 'For far too long,' she said—placing her hands on the table, the fingers bent and swollen as if they had been broken and badly reset—'we Britons have turned the other cheek.'

Winston listened to her speak, doubts pushing her words from his mind. How many people would they need to kill?

'Many lives will be lost,' she said, as if she knew what he was thinking. 'But we will prevail. This is our land. We should never give it up, nor hand it over. Can I trust you?'

'Yes, you can.'

'Resist the Islamists to your last breath. We need to make sure they never feel safe anywhere.' She stood up and walked away from the table. 'We will speak again tomorrow at midday.'

He watched her go, he didn't know what to say, or even what to call her: Shakespeare, the Jewess, HER: these were the names by which she was known, but they did not capture her commanding presence. Winston felt a mixture of awe and respect. An air of serenity surrounded her, of calmness and self-control; she emanated a steely determination but none of the raw ego and narcissism that normally surrounds those in power. She wasn't trying to impress, or act out a role. It was as if she could see straight into his heart and knew the pain he carried. She reminded him of his mother, of his home town, of the wheat country where he grew up, and the earth to which he would return. He admired the way she stood up to intimidation, despite being threatened and prosecuted and forced to flee her home. The Party had demonised her to such an extent that if she were to show her face on the streets above the mob would tear her to pieces.

She was the one who would take this country back. How she would achieve that goal he had no idea, it was simply a matter of faith. The alternative was too terrible to contemplate. Islamist corridors stretching from Cordoba to Gothenburg, from Lisbon to Prague. Fingers clasped his shoulder and he felt the breath of the blind man in his ear telling him how fortunate he was that Shakespeare had chosen to speak with him in person. What a great honour!

'I know,' he said.

The blind man leaned on his smart stick and stared up at the vaulted structure that was once part of a crumbling Norman church. 'Tomorrow is the day, God willing.' He spoke slowly without inflection as if he had learned the language in isolation.

'There's something I need to do first,' he said.

'What's that?'

'Visit someone.'

'I'm afraid that's not possible.'

The blind man removed his face covering and wiped sweat from his white beard. His features were Eurasian.

'I gave my word,' Winston said. 'Just one night.'

'I'm sorry. Nothing can be allowed to jeopardise our mission.'

'What *is* our mission?' Winston asked.

'You will be told when it is time. There are details to be settled. What is certain is you can't go back to your hostel. The IIS will be looking for you.'

'My passport, my clothes are still there.'

'We will get you a new passport. You can choose a different name.'

No, he liked Winston Smith. He'd grown used to it.

'Keeping Britain Safe' was the Party's motto. Despite the CCTV cameras, the drones and the electronic devices tracking every citizen's location, ordinary people felt no safer; all this surveillance merely increased their anxiety. If the IPGB could not guarantee security on the streets of London then eventually they would lose support. And yet Winston knew that killing people didn't change a thing. The Party could easily replace its motley army of muftis and imams, many of whom had little, or indeed any, formal education. Was it not more effective in the long term to challenge their ideas, to hold their ideology up to scrutiny, to expose their ignorance of science and technology, of music and art? And yet the Resistance had been left with little choice as the freedoms of what could be said or expressed or written in Britain had been whittled away. In the end, there was no other choice but violence.

'Have you spoken to anyone about us?'

'No-one,' he said. 'Why didn't they arrest me if I was under surveillance?'

'Because they wanted you to lead them to HER.'

'And have I?'

'There are hundreds and hundreds of these unmapped tunnels,' the blind man said. 'Most lead nowhere, many are blocked or too narrow for humans to pass through. The Intelligence Services never venture underground, they don't use dogs and they can't track us down here, so we are safe from their blackbirds.'

'Do me a favour,' Winston said. 'Speak to HER on my behalf.'

'I'm sorry. That's impossible.'

'Just ask HER. Please!' he said, pressing the tips of his fingers together. 'I'm begging you … just one night.'

The blind man stared at him; the pupils of his eyes were milky and strangely fixed. And then he turned and headed through the far door with the metal markings. Winston waited in the sunken baptistery. He was determined to find his way back to the surface. He had made up his mind to visit Chelsea and nothing they could do was going to prevent him. He couldn't survive down here, breathing in this mouldy dusty air, the atmosphere close and clammy. A world with no sun or moon was no world at all. Apart from a thin stream of clayish-brown water trickling through a drain, it was as quiet as the grave.

A wave of depression overcame him. It would take generations for this war to be won. Drops of moisture dropped onto the stone floor. He saw a sheet of paper and bent down to pick it up. It had a whorly texture and when he examined it closely he saw it was a piece of flayed human skin. He folded it into the pages of his notebook as the blind man emerged from behind the reinforced iron door and said, 'You have until midday tomorrow.'

'Thank HER for me.'

'Be careful, Mr Smith, they will be searching for you. Many ordinary decent Britons are now working for the IPGB. What choice do they have? Nowadays the best lack all conviction, while the worst are full of passionate intensity—'

'Yeats?' he said.

'And what rough beast, its hour come round at last,' the blind man whispered, 'slouches towards London to be born. The Second Coming is upon us.' And turning on his heels he took off in the opposite direction from which they had come.

Winston followed, amazed at how rapidly this old blind man was able to navigate the swerving tunnels. Head lowered, he seemed to know instinctively which turn to take and which entrance to avoid, despite there being no obvious markings along the walls. Smaller tunnels ran off everywhere, some stacked with cobwebbed coffins, others collapsed with bricks and blocked by iron gates. Weaving past crypts filled with moldering bones and galleries of faded murals, he could barely keep pace. Water sloshed around his shoes and twice he slipped on slimy old bricks and had to steady himself by clutching at the mossy walls. The blind man stopped in a narrow passageway and checked the readings on a hand-held instrument. 'All clear,' he said and nodded at a metal service ladder bolted into the brickwork. A dark shaft fell away at their feet while the ladder rose into the steamy darkness.

'What do I call you?' Winston said.

'Names are unimportant.'

'How many of us are there?'

'Millions,' the blind man said. 'Go now.'

He began to climb. Through a grating he heard the roar of a train passing somewhere above and felt its vibrations travel through the rungs to his fingers and up his forearms. Names and initials were carved into the walls and there was a date—September 1939. Was it possible the military had used this shaft during WWII? The country was at war again, only this war, unlike the last one, was undeclared. When he looked down the blind man was gone and he was climbing one hand after the other leaving the gloom of the underground bunker behind. He emerged through a manhole into a disused tube station, its walls covered with advertisements from a previous era showing happy-go-lucky couples driving low-slung Austin Healeys and Triumph convertibles, women with long black cigarette holders sipping fizzy drinks.

It was as if he'd travelled back through time. Faded oxblood tiles indicated this station was once part of the Circle Line. He followed the exit signs up some blackened steps past a retractable mesh gate and manoeuvred his way over coils of electrical cabling and then pushed on a splattered fire door that led to more steps and when he reached the top he came to a platform that was covered in old mattresses, fire blankets, torn sleeping bags and tattered fur coats laid down in rows, some even obscuring the tracks. Sticks of furniture had been dragged down here and propped against the walls, a bar fridge used as a cupboard and there were chairs and sofas of all shapes and sizes, some with the stuffing torn out of them and in the middle of this ghostly platform lay a circle of bricks. He squatted beside the ashy remnants of a fire and picked up a coat-hanger that had been twisted into a skewer for grilling meat.

Where was everyone? He could hear a noise coming from beyond the boarded-up windows, felt a tremor of sound reverberating through the tiles. He prised open a sheet of roofing iron, squeezed past rough-nailed timber planks blocking the exit and emerged into the blinding daylight. A rally was taking place outside a park and thousands of the faithful filled the streets waving banners and placards. Bearded men in long white gowns remonstrated with the heavens and women covered in chadors and abayas uttered a high-pitched ululation. Red buses decorated with posters bearing the words 'Subhan Allah' tooted their horns.

Fireworks exploded overhead and the roar of the crowd was like the rumble of an earthquake. Winston shuffled forward. The Grand Mufti stood on a spear-tipped balcony overlooking the large public park, motioning his hands in the air as if summoning the Ummah. The Party had stirred the resentments not only of the faithful but of all those who had lost out in society. For the poor, the destitute and the millions who had recently arrived from the drought and war-afflicted lands there existed a great sense of excitement. This was their victory. This was their time. The free movement of people across national boundaries was irreversible. Tomorrow was Saturday, the celebrations had begun, and London would never be the same.

# 7

Winston opened his notebook. It was important to write things down. He wondered if it would work to justify everything he did by saying God told him to do it. God told him to join the Resistance. God told him to kill Islamists. But instead of God he wrote Sarah for she had lured him into her world of activism and intrigue, indoctrinated him into her movement. Left to his own inertia he would still be teaching history in that western-suburbs high school, where on Diversity Day the headmaster proudly announced new segregated classes for boys and girls—citing data that students were more likely to achieve better academic results.

Sarah wasn't the type of woman who wanted to live a quiet married life in a small inner-city terrace. In those early days, the movement could not have survived without her. She was the one who organised the meetings, who ran their social media campaign, who petitioned politicians and warned the public about Jihadis. Every stabbing in Paris, every shooting in Brussels and Strasbourg only emboldened her to double her efforts. 'We are all Jews now,' she said, after the bombing of a synagogue in the Goutte d'Or.

'Who cares what happens elsewhere,' he said to her, 'why not live our lives peacefully. Life is short, let's enjoy each other's company, let the future take care of itself.' For her, love was not enough. Most likely he would have followed her anywhere, whatever her views. He didn't regard himself as being from the left or right. He was never an ideologue; only a witness to this moment in history. He was distrustful of causes and of the people who joined them.

'We have a simple choice,' she told him, 'resistance or submission'.

In the end it was he who stayed at home and minded Tess while Sarah devoted her energies to expanding their grassroots movement, tripling its membership and thereby gaining the attention of the security agencies who regarded her as far more dangerous than the Jihadis. 'Any culture that does not treat women as equals,' she told him, 'deserves to be destroyed.'

When he first joined the Resistance, Winston lost most of his friends. To have the conviction of your beliefs took enormous courage and no-one he'd known had more courage than Sarah. These days he tried not to think of her constantly, but it did no good. She was always lingering in the back of his mind. What he missed most was the touch of her hand on his chest, the sound of her breathing in bed, the warmth and smell of her olive skin. He'd needed to be told that she loved him. Needed to be convinced it was true. Yearning constantly for her affection.

He sat on the riverbank watching the barges and the barefoot children splashing about on the pier. He'd grown up in western Sydney near a river poisoned by heavy metals, where swimming and fishing were prohibited, but at least that river was blue.

He held the leather notebook up to the glancing light and studied the faint impressions left by its previous owner: 'Beautiful sunny day with little breeze. Weeded gooseberries, saw a buzzard carrying a large brown rat in its claws. Eric very sick in bed today, despairs of England and its intellectuals who despise their own culture.'

What would this woman say today? Who would she blame?

Winston snapped the notebook shut. Of course, it seemed so simple in retrospect, but who dared mention what was happening before the election? The Party encouraged the migrant influx in order to take over the host nation: whoever emigrates for the cause of Allah, they preached, will find on the earth many locations and abundance. They occupied the spiritual vacuum that existed at the heart of Europe and while its sclerotic leaders looked to the past the Party made plans for the future.

He got up and walked north on Southhampton Row, grime clinging to the pores of his skin, past a pack of topless boys with green headbands selling bottled water. Decaying Georgian houses smelt of spicy curries and leaking lavatories. He saw a vision of London, vast and ruinous, potholed and polluted, a city of broken sewer pipes and overflowing rubbish bins.

A well-built man wearing a tiger skin on his back and a wolf's head for a cap was holding out thin strips of coloured plastic. For all the interest he was getting he may as well have been flogging lumps of dirt but he smiled at Winston and called out *alsalamu alaikum*. On hoardings and walls, select sayings from the Qur'an were painted for the faithful to read, encouraging the hijrah. Who could deny the celebratory mood on the streets, the waving of streamers, the tooting of horns, the rejoicing that this country had finally chosen the righteous path?

Winston moved through the crush of pedestrians who spilled onto the road, forcing vehicles to go around them. From a stall he bought a bag of green apples, and stopped to scour the faces behind him. How would he know if someone was following him?

He found a Cocoa House near Russell Square run by two large African women. An armed guard stood in the doorway. It was rare to find genuine chocolate in Britain due to the world-wide shortage of cacao, although the fake synthetic stuff was readily available. Inside, small slabs of chocolate individually wrapped in gold leaf were arranged on silver trays. He held up one finger and the woman reached over with her tongs and grasped one of the tiny 10-gram bars then slipped it into a miniature bag and tied it with a green ribbon. It was as if he was buying a valuable piece of jewellery.

'That'll be thirty-four pounds,' she said, revealing cacao smears on her teeth.

He took his gift out into the street, sticking to the shadows so as to avoid the heat. Quickly, with an occasional wrong turn, he made his way through Bloomsbury to the crumbling Georgian terrace. A plaque on the wall stated that a distinguished Pakistani ambassador had once lived here. He walked past the house, scanning the upper windows. What if she wasn't home? What if her invitation to return was a trap?

Sunlight glinted off the chrome trim on a long black German saloon parked outside. What concerned him was her relationship to the owners of this three-storey Georgian house. What duties did she perform that allowed her to sleep in their coal cellar? She was more like a house pet than an au-pair. He strode across the street, ducked down the steps and rattled the iron mesh on her door. Chelsea opened it and ushered him inside, checking behind him to see if he was alone.

'Oh, my darling!' she said, as if she had learnt the words from a romance, 'I knew you'd come.' She took a step back and said, 'What's that muck on your face?'

He went over to the mirror above her sink and saw his nose and beard were smeared with black silt. The water from her tap was a brownish trickle but he scrubbed his hands and face. To think he had wandered the streets looking like this. She handed him a towel and asked how he'd gotten so dirty.

'Underground,' he said.

'So what have you brought me?'

He showed her the bag of green apples and her face fell. When he handed her the bar of chocolate she clapped her small hands with delight. She tore off the pretty foil packaging, snapped off a portion of dark chocolate and let it melt in her mouth. She moaned with pleasure.

'You must try this, Winston.'

'How do you know my name?'

'You told me.'

'Did I?' He couldn't remember.

'Is Winston your real name?'

'No,' he said. 'Is Chelsea yours?'

'Mum named me after the song.'

'What song?'

'Don't you listen to music?' She placed the remainder of chocolate on his tongue and he let it dissolve, savouring the rich smooth cocoa flavour. He could not recall ever tasting anything so good.

'You like it?' Her fingers tugged at his belt and he heard his buckle hit the floor. 'Let's get you out of these dirty clothes.' She unzipped his bomber jacket and stripped off his jeans and he caught a whiff of the tunnels he'd crawled through. 'What were you doing underground?' She pulled off his T-shirt. 'I got lost,' he said. She still wore that coarse over-garment but no safety scarf, and her hair was long and thick and oily to the touch. She unzipped her abaya and pulled it over her head. Underneath she wore a camisole and white briefs. She turned around, displaying her figure. 'What do you think? Did you dream about me?'

'Every night.' He stood before her in his underpants.

She took his hand and led him over to the bed. When they sat on the mattress, the springs squeaked in protest. She had scrounged pieces of mis-matched furniture, hung two coats and a feathery sunhat from nails on the wall and plastered photos of sunny Greek islands above her bed, but despite her attempts the room reminded Winston of a prison cell.

'Do you want sex?' she said.

Why not? Hadn't he come all this way? It had been a long while and he was so close, his knee touching hers. This was what he'd come for, the heat of her body, the swelling of her small firm breasts beneath her camisole, the soft touch of her skin. What a strange animal compulsion, this need for skin-to-skin contact. Chelsea pressed him down on the bed and their lips met. The bed squeaked again; they shifted position and it squeaked louder. 'Sorry about this,' she said. They pulled apart and tried nearer the foot of the bed but the squeaking persisted wherever they lay. 'Bloody bed,' she said.

He sat upright; all of a sudden the moment was gone. She rolled away from him and clasped her knees together under her chin.

'There's no rush, my dear. We've got all afternoon.' A tiny blue and red tattoo was freshly inked above her left ankle, the skin around it inflamed. 'You like my little bird?' she said. 'I got it for you.'

'Really?' Why would she get it for him? He disliked tattoos and weren't they illegal now?

'You told me you liked birds,' she said.

'Did I?' He couldn't remember saying such a thing, although it was true. It was something he'd noted since his arrival. No birds anywhere. All the common garden birds had disappeared, the warblers and robins, the sparrows and starlings.

'It's a blue tit,' she said. 'Isn't it sweet?'

When she smiled, she concealed her teeth with one hand. She got up, walked across the cellar in her camisole and briefs and leaned against the packing case. There was something about her he'd liked from the beginning, a brightness, a feigned indifference, or maybe just her youth. Whatever the reason, his brain had responded positively to her on the tube long before he was able to articulate the attraction.

'Take me with you,' she said.

'Where?'

'To Australia. I want to live in a country without Islamists.'

'We've got them there as well.'

'I hate them,' she said.

'What about the owner of this house? Surely he's a Party member?'

'Yes, but Sadiq is different. He's educated, he's generous, he respects women, he's not a fanatic.'

'Did you have sex with him?'

'Why do men always want to know who a girl's had sex with? Does it matter? Isn't the present more important than what happened sometime in the past?'

'The past is all we've got,' Winston said. 'The Party want to replace our past.'

'You're one of the terrorists, aren't you?'

He half expected her to panic, to run out the door and across the path to the main building. If she did he would not try to stop her. He would drop to his knees and place his hands behind his head.

'I knew it,' she said, 'I knew you were hiding something. Why does anyone travel halfway across the world if they're not a believer?' She crossed to the bed and clasped her arms around his neck. 'So why are you here?'

He looked up into her eyes.

'Are you going to kill someone?' she said.

'Yes, I am.'

She pulled away from him and strode over to the iron door. Stood there for a moment with her back towards him. Red lines marked her skinny thighs where she had leaned against the packing case. Why did he blurt it out? What possible reason was there to confide in Chelsea? All he had done was jeopardize her safety. She had no choice now but to inform the authorities. To even think of killing Islamists was a serious crime in England, but to say those words aloud was an act of terror, punishable by life imprisonment. Winston had never killed before, but he would do it with his bare hands if necessary. He owed his wife; he owed his daughter.

'How many are you going to kill?'

'As many as I can,' Winston said. He had rehearsed it in his mind: the surprise blow from behind, the frenzied attack in the high street, the rush of pure adrenalin. Oh yes, he could do it, he was perfectly capable of murder.

'And when do you plan to carry out this attack?' Chelsea asked.

'Once the Resistance gives me the order.'

'So the Resistance does exist?' She turned to face him with a look of excitement. 'I thought it was all propaganda, a ruse to keep us afraid... so there really is a Resistance?'

'There really is,' Winston said. 'And I've met HER.'

'That old Jewess on the wallscreen. Is she as evil as they say?' Chelsea walked over and picked his notebook off the floor. She opened it and ran her fingers slowly over the rubbed pages. Frown lines formed between her eyebrows. 'What's this?' she said.

Winston explained that it was a notebook; that in the past people used to write down things they did during the day.

'Why?' Chelsea asked. To her that was pointless. The government knew everything about you, they knew where you'd been, who you spoke to, even what products you bought; they listened in on your private conversations, they tracked your movements, so why would anyone need to write things down in a notebook?

He explained that in the past people liked to write down their thoughts.

'Hah!' Chelsea scoffed. That was even more stupid. 'The last thing you wanted was *them* knowing your thoughts.'

'Notebooks are private,' he told her. 'They aren't meant to be read by other people.' He took the notebook and began telling her about this amazingly resourceful English woman who lived a hundred years ago. She lived on a remote farm and raised chickens, planted crops and cared for a man so ill and weak he was barely able to lift a hand to pull out a weed.

Chelsea examined the pencil marks. 'If notebooks were so private, then how come you've got hers?'

'I bought it in a second-hand shop. Would you like to read it?'

She shook her head.

'Why not?' he said. Perhaps she was illiterate or perhaps it was something else. He looked around the converted cellar. Surprisingly there was no wallscreen, no electronic devices of any kind. Next to the antique turntable a stack of her 45s lay in their brown paper sleeves. A thin mattress, a pair of discoloured sheets and a few coarse army blankets made up her squeaky bed. Compared to hundreds of thousands of Londoners who slept rough each night, Chelsea was fortunate to have a roof over her head, but how was she able to afford it?

'You don't have a wallscreen,' he said. 'That's unusual. Tell me about your friend in the house.'

'Sadiq? If it wasn't for Sadiq I'd be sleeping on the streets.'

'So why does he help you?'

'Because he has two young daughters,' she said.

Winston stared at her small pale face. He trusted her and yet he was suspicious just the same.

'You think I'm a spy?' She pulled up her camisole to expose her breasts. 'See, no hidden cameras.' She tugged it down defiantly. 'Besides, they would never enlist someone like me, white, female and promiscuous.'

She had a point. The female sexual impulse was considered dangerous by the Party. Keeping women in purdah was important to them.

'I have a lot of sexual thoughts,' she said. 'Don't you?'

'Listen to this,' Winston read: 'Beautiful English day. Sea glassy smooth. Picked mulberries early this morning, large and delicious—'

'What are mulberries?' Chelsea said.

'Took boat out and caught three fish for dinner, saw a flight of thrushes, rare sight. Pigs getting through wire netting—'

'Pigs are illegal,' Chelsea interrupted.

'Not back then,' he told her. 'Transplanted raspberry suckers, sowed winter spinach. Drove seventeen miles to town to post off manuscript. Mended puncture on the way & two more on the way home.'

'Why are you reading me this stuff?' she said.

'Because this woman kept a notebook shortly after the war when the country had just defeated the Nazis and the future was full of promise.' He put down the notebook and the dried piece of human skin floated onto the floor. Chelsea picked it up between her fingers and examined it closely. 'You really are strange. Are all Australians like you?'

'No.'

'Why this obsession with the past?'

'The past is all we have,' he said.

'No, the past is dead. It's only now that matters.'

'But you like old records?' He took the layer of human skin back and slipped it into his notebook.

'But that's music, not digging around in the frozen hard ground for vegetables. My Nan scrubbed floors all her life for rich people so I don't get dreamy about the good old days. Men love to tell us women that we're free to do what we want, but for our own safety we have to do what we're told.'

He got down on his knees and searched under her bed.

'You won't find any listening devices under there.'

He asked if she had a spanner and she rummaged around in a box of tools next to her packing case and pulled out an adjustable wrench. He used it to tighten the bolts on the side rails of the bed. When he finished, Chelsea jumped onto the bed and wriggled out of her underwear. He climbed in under the sheets beside her. Her body was warm and inviting. 'What are you doing?' he said. She told him it was a security frisk.

'OK, you're clean,' she said and laughed. She pressed him down on the bed and her toes locked into his. This time there was no squeaking.

The sex was as good as he remembered. Why didn't people make love day and night and forget about everything else? This was the closest he came to God. She called out, raw animal sounds rather than words, her throat flushed, a film of sweat forming between her breasts then bending low she kissed him tenderly. She was a good kisser, and then they rolled apart. Afterwards, she lay there in the crook of his arm with her head heavy on his chest and her hand hooked over his hip and for a long while they did not speak.

'I love sex,' she whispered, 'I love it more than anything—'

'More than chocolate?'

'Apart from chocolate,' she said. 'I want other girls my age to know that sex is O.K. We don't have to be ashamed of our desires.'

She sat up and played with her stringy hair. It occurred to him that he didn't even know this young woman's surname, and yet he understood that her sexual bravado was not an act but a form of defiance. How many other men had she brought back here in exchange for chocolates or money and yet her promiscuity didn't bother him, quite the contrary, it made her more appealing. She did what she liked with her own body and took her pleasure unashamedly. Life, she explained, was fleeting, and she compared herself, rather vainly, to an English butterfly, flitting from flower to flower, intending to fit in as much fun as she could in her short life span. The Islamists were against fun, she said, they were against music. 'They want us women to be chaste and shining with virtue,' Chelsea said with disgust.

'So you're not working for them?'

'I would rather die in a ditch,' she said. Any day she expected to be arrested for immoral behaviour. She had received her second repentance card from the SIPs and feared being sent to prison or worse—to one of the new female rehabilitation centres. It was only a matter of time before they got to her.

He sat up and put his arm around her waist and Chelsea rested her head on his shoulder. Her scalp smelled of lye soap; her hair was knotted and wild. He didn't want to think of the future, there was no future for either of them only this brief moment of intimacy, and yet he felt not only affection for her but also a sense of admiration. Soon they would part and never set eyes on each other again. It gave him hope that there were still young women in London like Chelsea. He looked around her cellar. Millions of Britons were now homeless, but millions more were living like this in cramped, damp, unsanitary conditions. The tattoo on Chelsea's ankle looked infected; it didn't resemble a real bird, it was more like a rough cartoon, perhaps the tattooist had never seen a living bird. It stirred in him a memory of watching a family of Superb Fairy-wrens that had nested in their Sydney backyard. Sarah tried to entice them to stay by leaving out shallow containers of water beneath the prickly grevilleas but they were gone within weeks. An insignificant memory, but at that time they both perceived these little hopping birds as an augury of love.

'You want to hear some music?' Chelsea said. She went over to the packing case, flipped through her 45s, selected a disc and placed it on the turntable. 'I always like to hear music after sex, don't you?'

'Not really,' he said. He preferred silence.

Chelsea folded her naked body in beside him listening to the mournful voice of a female soul singer. He didn't ask who it was and she didn't tell him, but he felt her lips move in sync with the words. When the song had finished she lifted the needle off the scratchy record and wiped a tear from her eyes. She took a small green apple from the bag and came back to bed crunching it noisily. 'Such a sad song,' she said, in between bites. 'This man and a woman fall in love, then he goes off to war and dies.'

'And what happens to her?' he said.

'Oh, she finds someone else, but she always remembers him. You're married aren't you, Winston?'

He explained that his wife and daughter were killed in the triple attacks.

'Oh, I'm so sorry,' she said. 'What was she like, your wife?'

'She was kind, she was loving, she was determined, she was infuriating, and she was courageous. She was everything a good woman can be. There was nothing I didn't love about her and that's rare, because there's always some little thing.' He never understood what Sarah saw in him; she could have had any man she wanted and yet she chose a humble history teacher. Was it because he was so ordinary, or was it because he was loyal? Or was there something else in him that only she saw?

'Was she pretty?' Chelsea said.

'Yes.'

'Prettier than me?'

'I wouldn't like to compare.'

'So she was, wasn't she? And you still love her, don't you?' Chelsea said, tossing her gnawed apple core onto the floor. 'What did you love about her?'

'I loved her body, I loved being with her.'

'Sexually, you mean?'

'Anywhere,' he said. 'I loved her, and sometimes she loved me too.'

She turned to study him. 'I've never met anyone from the Resistance before. I remember after the triple attacks my Nan got religion. Everyone did. You'd think fanatics blowing up thousands of innocent people would turn everyone off religion, but here it had the opposite effect. I guess they didn't want what happened to those American cities to happen here.'

'It was the same in Australia,' he said. 'The Americans spent trillions protecting their homeland from attack when all along the sleeper squads had penetrated inside the wall.'

Lying beside her with one hand clasping her small firm breast, he understood how easy it would be to accept things, to convince yourself that all that mattered was your own little space, to turn your back on the outside world, to let it all go to hell.

He could feel Chelsea's ribs underneath her skin and her sharp angular body burrowing into his gave him hope that there might be a future for them. This was their world now and he would rather die above ground than live like a dung beetle below. She did not resemble Sarah on any level but she was warm and genuine and in the afternoon light slanting through the barred window he stared at her small pale face.

'Don't stare at me,' she said. 'I'm not an insect.'

'I want to remember what you look like,' he said. 'You're beautiful. I'm 33 years old and my hair is falling out. What do you see in me?'

'Take me with you, Winston.'

'Where?'

'Anywhere. I can give you information.'

'What kind of information?'

'Warnings, things a person might need to know.'

From the street came the sound of horns and drums beating. The Dhol players were leading the celebrations.

The smell of her body and the firmness of her hand between his thighs made him feel secure. He fell asleep wondering what it would be like to carve out an existence for the two of them in a remote corner of Scotland, a man and a woman tilling the soil and eking out a living from the land.

When he woke it was with that sense of unease that comes from having slept through an afternoon. Momentarily he had no idea of where he was but the sight of Chelsea stretched out beside him, naked, mouth open, revealing the decayed state of her teeth, brought him back to the present. Poor girl. Even if you tried to live outside society you still needed its basic services. The light was fading and he did not know what hour it was. His plan, if he could call it that, was to remain here overnight and then in the morning make his way by foot to Covent Garden and find the blind man. Tomorrow's attack on the Islamists must go ahead. It was too late to bail out now. The idea of starting life on a remote farm was no more than a fanciful notion. How long would it take before they starved to death or turned on one another? Unlike the woman in his notebook he had no knowledge of farming. He was a foreigner and Chelsea was a Londoner who survived on the edges with no apparent friends or family, apart from her Nan. A faint light pulsed from her turntable. He watched it, mesmerized by the intermittent blinking.

He sat up. He went over to the turntable and peered underneath. His heart began to pound and he felt a sense of dread. He stared at Chelsea lying on her bed, a tangle of dark hair and pale limbs. Either she had no idea they were being watched or else she had betrayed him. He shook her roughly. 'What?' she said, rubbing her eyes. He indicated the pinpoint of blue light. Her eyes widened. She knew what it was: a mini-cam they called the Eye of Allah. No bigger than a bush tick and magnetized, it recorded both image and sound.

'They know,' Chelsea whispered.

'Everything,' he said.

'What can we do?'

'Nothing.' He squeezed her hand. Finally, it had happened. It was only ever a matter of time and strangely he felt a sense of relief combined with an apprehension of what was to come. He had let down the Resistance in order to spend the night with a young woman he barely knew; he had no reason to trust her and yet trust her he did.

There was a violent banging at her door and Chelsea jumped out of bed with fright. 'Winston Smith?' a male voice called. The iron door flew open and five masked men wearing multi-terrain camouflage jackets rushed into the cellar. One of them wore a wolf's head for a cap and Winston recognized him as the beggar from the street. 'On your knees, kuffar,' he shouted. Winston dropped to the floor, but Chelsea stood there, trembling. 'Cover your aurat,' the man spat, 'don't you have any shame?' And taking two quicks steps he slapped her face so hard the blow echoed like a gunshot. Winston began to stand and a boot thudded into the base of his spine. He fell forward and a knee pinned his head to the floor and another man stood with his full bodyweight across the back of his legs. He could not move a muscle, his mouth pressed into the filthy floor. Chelsea cried out as two men grabbed her, twisting her arms and holding her down. Winston could not see what they were doing, but he heard her loud sobbing breaths. When they'd finished, they ransacked the cellar, ripping her tattered Greek postcards from the walls, smashed her packing case and antique turntable and then crushed her records one by one under their boots. A knife clanged on the stone floor and he heard Chelsea call, 'Please, Sadiq!' The man with the wolf's head cap barked a command and Winston felt the pressure lift off his neck. He glanced up at a silvery-haired man who had just entered. For some reason he expected to see Mr Warwick the bookseller or Mr Hoque or more likely Marlon transformed into some high-ranking IIS operative, but he'd never set eyes on this short, cold-eyed fish before. Wearing a navy suit with a red silk handkerchief bursting from his breast pocket and an open-neck white shirt, he gave a little bow. With his cufflinks and polished wingtips, he resembled a successful city investment banker rather than a feared IIS officer. 'Please accept my apologies, Mr Smith, for this sudden intrusion.' His accent was typically British, high-pitched.

'Why are you doing this, Sadiq?' Chelsea begged. 'Make them stop.'

With a snap of his fingers, Sadiq indicated for Chelsea to be removed and it was only then that Winston saw what they had done to her: her scalp was bleeding from cuts and nicks where they had shorn her roughly with a long-curved knife; chunks of her dark hair lay curled on the floor. Two of the men bundled her out of the cellar wrapped in a bedsheet with spittle hanging off her chin looking like some escaped mental patient, and when her eyes met his he recognized that look of helplessness and knew she would never be the same again.

'You want to avenge her, don't you, Mr Smith?' Sadiq said. The man with the wolf's head for a cap grinned; the other two men folded their arms.

Nobody showed any identification but there was no need. The Islamic Intelligence Services operated with impunity. They did not answer to judges or courts only to the Grand Mufti himself and to the laws handed down by Allah. Once the IIS had hold of you there was no hope of appeal. Your life was finished. If you were fortunate you might die of a heart attack while being interrogated but more likely you would rot for years in the notorious Belmarsh prison. 'What will happen to her?' he said.

'She will be charged with committing acts incompatible with public decency.' Sadiq stroked his neatly trimmed stubble. 'Women like her are no better than wild animals,' he said. 'They have no morality.'

'Let her go,' Winston said, 'and I'll tell you everything.'

'Come now, Mr Smith,' Sadiq said with a wry smile. 'We know everything already. We know about the tunnels, we know about the Jewess and we know about the attack planned for tomorrow's Parade.'

'So what do you want from me?'

'We don't want anything, Mr Smith.' The two men gripped his arms on either side and marched him out to the sleek black saloon parked in the street. The smell of liniment on their muscled bodies made him blink and forget to duck his head as they rammed him into the back seat. 'Be careful with our guest,' Sadiq said sharply. 'I'm afraid you are at a serious disadvantage, Mr Smith, because you know nothing about me, and yet I know everything there is to know about you.'

The man with the wolf's head cap grinned at him from the front seat, and whether it was the blow to his temple or the boot to the base of his spine, Winston began to feel dizzy. Time and space were distorted and as the black saloon pulled away from the kerb, he had the sensation that he was falling from the top of a very tall building.

# 8

Everything had changed and the world was filled with darkness. The light that once found its way in through the cracks was gone. It was impossible to see his hands held in front of his eyes. The only sound he heard was the sound of his own breathing. He had no watch, no book, no scrap of paper; they had removed his notebook, his trousers, his shoes and belt and left him in this sub-basement chamber no bigger than a prison cell. It stank of vomit. He suspected they were watching him through infra-red cameras.

He started to worry about his time on earth, how he had achieved nothing other than having loved. They could not take that away from him. If only Sarah and Tess hadn't gone to America. That was the hardest thing to come to terms with: the loss of his wife and child and the realisation of his own insignificance. You lived and you died and that was the end of it. All the trivial things a parent remembers become more important than anything else. Winston started singing to himself a silly little tune his 5-year-old daughter had liked, he wondered if she could hear, and then he burst into tears.

Without light, he could not maintain control of his emotions. There was no coherent pattern to his thoughts, images appeared and disappeared, groups of neurons firing off electrical signals. He had no means of estimating how much time had passed. He dozed for what might have been minutes but may as well have been hours. Squatting like an animal in the darkness, he began to hallucinate. He saw his daughter's tiny feet when she was born, held them in the palm of his hand, blueish, wrinkled with creases, marvelling at her toes. How beautiful, how staggeringly beautiful! What was happening to him? Was he losing his mind? He tried not to think. Too much thinking was not only dangerous but also depressing. The Islamists were right. They had taken charge of his thoughts. They were breaking him down. Resistance was futile. Submission was what they demanded. Submission to Allah. Submission to the Party. Winston felt nothing but numbness, as though he were losing the will to live. He got up and paced the concrete floor of the basement cell at number 80 Strand, where the clocks showed the time in Mecca.

There was no escape. Death was his only ride out. A woman screamed, a blood-curdling scream that froze him in his tracks. The screaming was coming from the ceiling. He'd never heard a woman in such pain, whatever they were doing to her, she was screaming over and over for them to stop. Please! He held his hands to his ears. He hoped his wife and daughter hadn't suffered like this; from what he'd learned, their deaths were instantaneous, blown to pieces in that Jewish supermarket in Atlanta. The Great Catastrophe. How many people had died at the hands of the jihadis in the triple attacks?

Moments of silence were followed by waves of screams piped through concealed speakers. It was Chelsea, he was sure of it. Whatever they were doing to her was so inhumane, that he could not begin to imagine it. The screaming erupted again and he screwed his fingers tightly into his ears. There were a handful of Resistance fighters who could hold out for two, three days, but eventually even the hardiest of them would break, and Winston was no hero. He understood they wanted to drive him to insanity until he begged them on his hands and knees to confess. The walls were closing in around him. The darkness had won. 'Enough!' he yelled. 'No more!'

The screaming stopped, or at least he could no longer hear it through the speakers, and the steel door opened. The light came in and he covered his eyes with his forearm blinking down at his besocked feet. The shapes of two men emerged through the doorway: Sadiq, followed by the thickset guard with the wolf's head cap. Winston stared at the shorter man's silvery hair swept back, the pious stubble. His brain had slowed as if to compensate for the lack of stimuli and the shiny buttons on Sadiq's jacket seemed to soak up all his focus.

'So Mr Smith, I wanted you to have time to think about your situation.'

'The girl,' he said. 'Did you torture her?'

'We don't torture, Mr Smith. We are not animals.'

'I heard a woman screaming—'

'Sometimes the mind plays tricks,' Sadiq said.

'You're saying I imagined her screams?'

'I can't tell you what you heard or did not hear. What I can say is that my duty is to protect society from immorality and unlawfulness.'

'What have you done to Chelsea?'

'Chelsea is not her real name, Mr Smith, just as Winston Smith is not your real name.' He spoke politely, enunciating his words and smiling in a friendly but sinister way. 'What is your purpose here in London?'

'You know my purpose.'

'To murder innocent women and children is that correct? So what makes you the hero in your own story?'

Winston stared at the guard with the wolf's head cap who seemed bored by all this small talk. It was obvious from his body language and steely glare that his preference was for a more direct approach, yet

Winston knew the worst kind of interrogators were those who were courteous and polite.

Sadiq said, 'We know about your wife and daughter Mr Smith, but we are not responsible. Prime Minister Nawaz has condemned those attacks, this is not our way, our path is success through the democratic process. The Americans are different with their electoral college, their second amendment and their gun-carrying evangelicals. Violence is the only answer there, but here in Britain we have achieved our victory legally and with very little bloodshed. I make no excuses for what occurred in those three cities but if successive U.S. administrations did not oppress Muslims and plunder our oil and invade our lands and mock our beliefs and belittle our women then perhaps there might not have been a need for such revenge attacks. Who can say with certainty? You are a teacher of history, Mr Smith. What has your discipline taught you about the past?'

'History is written by the victors.'

'Precisely. Since Tariq ibn Ziyad crossed the Straight of Gibraltar, Islam has always been a part of Europe, and always will be.'

'No, it hasn't,' he said, 'not since Philip of Spain expelled the Moors.'

'History is what we say it is, Mr Smith, not what you think it was. There is no such thing as your truth. There is only our truth.'

'Why not take what the West offers, why not be content with that?'

'Because the world has changed, Mr Smith. Look around you.'

'What do you want from me?' Winston said. He needed urgently to use the toilet.

'My father was born in the tribal areas of Pakistan and my mother in Swindon. When I was at Eton they sneered at me, this half-Pakistani boy. I have a Masters degree in chemical engineering from Cambridge so I am more English than the English, but we are all Muslims today. I want you to understand this city is ours just as much as Karachi or Riyadh. It is the will of Allah.'

Winston cast a glance at the hole in the concrete floor. Was that the latrine? With the guard blocking the doorway, there was insufficient light for Winston to see clearly. His stomach rumbled and he clenched his bowels. He would not humiliate himself.

'We know everything about you, Mr Smith. We know your real name. We know the reason you were selected for this mission.'

'Tell me,' he said, 'I'd like to know.'

'The changing ethnic composition of our capital caused a large exodus of people of no colour from London. With your mixed heritage they assumed you might fit in. Their old England has gone, but don't feel bad for it was a grimy little place, full of snobbery and prejudice. Be on the right side of history, Mr Smith, and you will come to thank us in time, I know it.'

'What will happen to Chelsea?' he said.

'That depends on you, I'm afraid. Your little friend has served her usefulness. She claimed she was a free spirit, free to do whatever she wished, but she was only free to do what we wished. That is the illusion of freedom, Mr Smith. No-one is ever really free.'

Winston said nothing; there was nothing to say.

The blades of Sadiq's thin lips flashed. 'If you want to save your young friend from further punishment,' he said, 'you will need to co-operate.'

He could not save his wife and daughter but he could swap his own life for Chelsea's on condition that his death was not drawn out. Avoidance of pain is what he aimed for. No doubt she was suffering. He didn't love her but he was willing to betray the Resistance if he could save her. He didn't know why. All he knew was that if you betray those you care for then you betray everything worthwhile. 'Alright,' he said. 'I'll take you to HER.'

'Good,' Sadiq said. 'I shall give you a moment to relieve yourself.' And with a click of his fingers he ordered the guard to manhandle

Winston from the cell and down a basement corridor. The light was so bright that he kept his head lowered, eyes squinting at the cracked-tiled floor. Party members wearing dark suits and open-neck shirts passed, none wearing a tie, and then a column of workers wearing sanitary clothing and blue surgical masks. There was no sign of Chelsea or any other prisoners but he saw a row of identical cells with their steel doors numbered. The guard jabbed him in the liver and propelled him into a white-walled windowless cell. This one was fluorescent lit and to his relief contained a lavatory and stainless-steel hand-basin, along with three giant wallscreens and a metal bunk on which hung his trousers.

Desperately, he squatted on the pan while the guard with the wolf's head cap stood in the doorway registering his disgust. He flushed and washed his hands. His shoes were missing but at least he had found his pants. He sat on the bed and the guard yelled at him to stand and when he stood the guard yelled at him to stand on the spot marked with a yellow X.

What seemed like a long time passed. He stood in the middle of the cell, the ceiling so low it scraped his head. The smell of dust lingered in the air. If these walls could speak they would scream. He thought of all the atheists and apostates who had passed through here since the election twelve months ago. Under the Malicious Communications Act, the Party had criminalized 'the sending or receiving of any electronic message that might be deemed un-Islamic'. In one year the IPGB had tightened its grip on power, made revolutionary changes and introduced hundreds of new laws and regulatory edicts, arresting anyone who dared question their legitimacy.

It was the blasphemy laws which had changed Britain forever. That's what everyone said. Introduced under the previous Unity government to promote global civility, the legislation was so broad and so loosely defined it allowed them to arrest and incarcerate anyone they wished. All that were required were two male witnesses. Aided and abetted by these new laws, which made criticism of religion 'a hate crime', the Party had won power in a landslide. Already they had established the Committee for the Promotion of Virtue, which monitored calls and electronic messages for 'obscene and blasphemous content'. The number of people imprisoned under the revised penal code for insulting, offensive or hostile speech had tripled. For every criticism levelled at them, the Party could point to an array of alternative facts demonstrating how much progress was being made in social cohesion, law and order, and the enforcement of moral decency. Sexual assaults were down, along with acid and terror attacks. The building of mosques in England and Wales was at an all-time high.

Sadiq appeared in the doorway, smiling, his polished brogues catching the light. He held the red leather notebook in the air: 'You wrote these words?'

Winston said nothing; the guard glared at him.

'I despise the Islamists …' Sadiq read slowly. 'Theirs is a primitive ideology … it robs men, women and children of their free will … Is this your writing, Mr Smith?'

Before he could reply the guard took two quick steps and slapped his face so hard his nose began to bleed.

Sadiq continued softly: 'Radical Islam is a religion for slaves, fearful, intolerant ... Did you write these words?'

Winston's head was still ringing from the guard's slap. 'I might have,' he stammered, 'I'm not sure …' The servile tone in his own voice made him feel ashamed. He was glad Sarah was not present to witness his cowardice, but she was dead and he was still clinging to … what exactly … he didn't know.

'I despise its sheer stupidity!' Sadiq said. 'You wrote this poison?'

The guard leapt forward and smashed him under the sternum with so much force Winston crashed to the ground gasping. His diaphragm spasmed in pain. Sadiq ignored the low animal sounds that escaped from his lips as if they had no connection with him or his bodyguard.

'Incitement of religious mockery and hatred against the Islamic Party of Great Britain is a very serious crime. In fact, there is no more serious crime. The right to freedom of thought and expression can never justify blasphemy.'

Winston nodded, blood dripping from his nose. Nothing had prepared him for this. He stayed down in case the guard struck him again. All those years of talking in front of a class, expressing his thoughts freely. He wanted to point out that his notebook was private, but thought better of it.

'I am giving you an opportunity, Mr Smith, to explain yourself. Did you write these words?'

'Yes,' he said.

'So we have a confession. And where did you acquire your pseudonym, Mr Smith?'

'From a book. We studied it at school.'

'And do you recall what happened to that other Winston Smith?'

'His spirit was crushed.'

'He came to love Big Brother just as you will come to love the Party and the Prophet, May Peace Be Upon Him. Your remarks are born of ignorance. When you write that our faith is primitive and intolerant don't you see how hurtful that is?'

The guard stepped forward and slapped his cheek but it had none of the ferocity of the previous blow and was more a reminder. Winston's mouth was dry and a sharp pain worked inside his abdomen. He stood up and wiped his nose on his arm. Sadiq leaned back, careful not to soil his crisp white shirt. 'Did we not win the last election?' he said. 'Have we not proven our democratic right to govern this country? You think we are unkind, but no, we are merciful. That does not give you permission to express vile and hateful things. Writing is a filthy habit.' Sadiq waved the notebook in the air—its spine was broken and loose pages flew onto the floor. He motioned to the guard to pick them up and said, 'Tell me Mr Smith, did you really believe this was Avril Blair's notebook?'

'Whose?'

'Avril Blair's. Surely you knew Eric Blair had a sister?'

'No, I didn't,' he said.

'But you knew the woman's name in the notebook was Avril and the invalid typing his manuscript in bed was named Eric. Who did you assume he was?'

'I don't know,' he said. 'I didn't think of anyone in particular.'

'You disappoint me, Mr Smith. A teacher of history.'

'Ancient History,' he said.

'We know what you taught. We know everything about you, so I am surprised you didn't know George Orwell had a younger sister who cooked and cleaned and nursed him in his final days. Without her, Orwell would not have completed his major work. She was his essential companion until he checked into Cranham sanitorium. Avril Blair did everything for her big brother in those last months of his life except write his book.'

'I wasn't attempting to uncover her identity,' he said. 'I was more interested in her observations about nature and the land.'

'We thought you would enjoy those little details.' Sadiq read from a page: 'Picked wild blackberries, planted yellow crocuses …' He smiled and exchanged a glance with the guard.

'What do you mean?' Winston said.

'We planted that notebook. One of our intelligence officers copied out passages from Avril Blair's personal notebooks in pencil, then rubbed the entries out lightly. The difficulty was in making the paper and leather binding look suitably aged.'

'Why go to all that trouble?'

'It was no trouble, Mr Smith, it was part of our plan.'

'I don't understand. How did you know I would buy it?'

Sadiq spoke gently, as if he were explaining a simple algebra equation to a child: 'We have steered you like a goat from the moment you touched down at Heathrow. You think you are master of your own fate, but you are not. What do you believe in, Mr Smith? Do you believe in God?'

'No.'

'What then?'

'I believe in free will.'

Sadiq laughed, revealing his back teeth. 'Really?'

'Yes,' he said. 'We determine our own fate, we make our own decisions in life.'

'There is no free will, Mr Smith. Everything that has happened to you in London has been orchestrated by us—by the party of Allah. Free will is a myth.'

'That's not true,' he said.

Sadiq smiled wearily as if Winston was a slow learner. 'We know everything about you Mr Smith or should I call you Mr Johnson. That is your real name, George Johnson. I think I prefer Winston Smith. How unimaginative your parents must have been?' He sighed and took several paces across the basement cell. The guard looked on.

'You chose the name Winston Smith, didn't you? Think carefully. Or was it chosen for you?'

Winston had a vague memory of someone in Sydney suggesting that he use the name. Was it O'Connell?

'Was it not your large Irish friend?'

It was O'Connell who suggested he take the name, yes it was O'Connell who had told him the Resistance needed someone 'ordinary' who could pass through customs and immigration undetected, 'travel under the radar', were the exact words he used, and take a message to HER.

He went to step forward but the guard intervened, motioning for him to remain standing on the yellow X. 'O'Connell's not working for you?' he said in disbelief.

Sadiq smiled in his well-bred English way. 'You are not the first Winston Smith to pass through London thinking you are cleverer than the Party. Do we look like fools? You borrow a character's name from a well-known book of fiction, and you think we won't notice?'

Sadiq was right. The false name was O'Connell's idea. And that business at Heathrow with the immigration officer? Now he realized they had deliberately let him through, kept him under close surveillance, watched him like a fly trapped in a jar.

'You see what distinguishes us from you,' Sadiq said, 'is our belief in Al-Qadar. What this means is that everything in our lives is already written. It is our duty to know that whatever Allah wills will occur. He is the creator of everything including all our deeds. Allah knows our past, present and future, just as we know yours, Mr Smith. Our lives are set, but that does not mean that we strive any less towards perfection.'

'What value is there in living life like a slave?' Winston said.

'It is not us who are the slaves.' Sadiq straightened his pocket handkerchief. 'You delude yourself if you think otherwise.'

'Did Chelsea know about this?'

'Poor Chelsea. She has no comprehension of the real world. We arranged for you two to meet on the tube and then to cross paths in the street. Your relationship, your entire attachment to each other was pre-arranged.'

'I don't believe you,' he said. 'Why bother interrogating me if you know everything?'

'Because we knew you would lead us to the Jewess. Your Resistance cannot win. We are too many, too strong and we have belief. You have nothing. Only things. One day all of Europe will be ours. That is not a boast, that is a fact. You are a dead culture but we will give you life.'

The guard stiffened, a look of intensity in his dark eyes. Armed men strode down the corridor, the ringing of boots on concrete. An announcement came over the speakers but Winston couldn't make out the words.

'Do you know when Orwell—and, like you,' Sadiq continued softly, 'that was not his real name. Do you know when Eric Blair finished *Nineteen Eighty-Four*, or *The Last Man in Europe* as he was inclined to call it, Muslims made up one sixth of the World's population. Today they make up more than one quarter and growing. What does that tell you, Mr Smith? That Orwell's prediction of three totalitarian super-states never eventuated. What he didn't count on was the inextinguishable belief in Allah. Orwell failed to understand that as a way of life Islam is far superior to the failed ideologies of communism and socialism.'

Winston listened, asking himself why Sadiq liked talking so much. Was it because he enjoyed the sound of his own voice? Was he the future and men like Winston the past?

'The West is dying, Mr Smith. Orwell had it profoundly wrong. Socialism did not win. Communism did not win. What Orwell didn't realize was the importance of religion in the lives of the proletariat. It is the cement that binds the disparate races together. Without it Europe is lost, a collection of old buildings and crumbling bridges. Do you know there are fewer atheists in the world today than there were fifty years ago? In Orwell's time over half the world's population was socialist or communist. And today—how many communist countries exist? Apart from China, one or two failed rogue states. More than ever people need religion, they need hope that this short animal existence is not all there is, there cannot just be this life and then nothing.'

Winston listened to the emotion in Sadiq's voice, watched the waving of his index finger. The guard stroked his untamed beard and when Sadiq uttered key words, Islam, Kuffar, Allah, the guard's eyes grew fiery.

'What does a true socialist hope for, Mr Smith—the equality of man, the redistribution of wealth? Abstractions, things that never existed and will never exist. What does a capitalist wish for? The latest Italian supercar, a new mistress. What socialism and capitalism have in common is a spiritual emptiness. We live and we die, that is unfair is it not? A waste of our knowledge and experience, why can't there be an afterlife?'

'Because it's not real,' Winston said.

'People don't seek reality, Mr Smith. Your name is not real and yet you cling to it regardless. People want hope, they pine to belong, they yearn to believe. Does the present matter so much if the future contains our wildest dreams?'

'What about freedom?' he said.

'Really, you disappoint me, Mr Smith. Freedom is the most misused word in the English language. Are you free? Is Britain free?'

'No,' Winston said.

'Was it ever truly free? Remember Orwell's three groups: the High, the Middle and the Low. Of course, he was referring to England, where the Low, the great majority of people, are crushed by drudgery. Britain was never free, Mr Smith, but at least it can be great again. We will convert your empty churches into places of worship. We will turn democracy on its head. Who can deny us our rights? We have set the standard for other parties across Europe to follow. A majority of Britons voted for my Party and a minority of malcontents like your Jewess refuse to accept the verdict. Who are the terrorists now, Mr Smith?'

The guard muttered a prayer to himself. Winston clutched his abdomen, his thoughts flying about wildly.

With an air of great satisfaction, Sadiq continued: 'To be honest, I found *Nineteen Eighty-Four* rather dull—the prose is pedestrian, Airstrip One is nothing more than a projection of post-war London with its food rations and bombed-out buildings. And Orwell never provides us with a sense of a living, thriving metropolis, a massive urban population like we have in London today, but my main objection is that everyone is so stupid, the Proles, the Workers, the Party Members, it is an unbelievably bad book. And that long dreary sequence by Goldstein on *The Theory and Practice of Oligarchical Collectivism*. Did you skip that part too?'

'I don't recall,' Winston said.

'I'm sure you did. No matter. I prefer *Animal Farm*. You see,' Sadiq said, with a reassuring smile, 'mankind invented God for a reason, but when mankind's invention proved incapable of solving all our problems, the West's intellectuals tried to uninvent him. But there was one critical thing they failed to comprehend and it is this: once you have thought of God you can never unthink him.'

A sense of helplessness washed over him. Even if it were possible to break out of his cell and roam the streets where could he go? London was a prison with parks and trains and the Islamists were its gaolers.

'No-one can save you. That is what you were thinking, am I right? We are aware of every crime you have committed, every blasphemous thought, and yet we are willing to spare you because we are the best of Allah's creations. We want you to work for us.'

'And if I refuse?' Winston said meekly.

'Your little bird will be crushed.'

Betraying the Resistance meant betraying everything he believed in. He barely knew Chelsea, he didn't love her, he had slept with her once, but at least she was alive, unlike his wife and daughter. What choice did he have?

'You have no choice,' Sadiq said, with a knowing smile.

He stared at the confident face: was it possible Sadiq could read his mind? He tried to focus on his immediate surroundings: the murkish light seeping down the corridor, a low hum of machinery. 'What am I thinking now?' he said.

Sadiq gave a different smile. He had half a dozen smiles, each one indicating his superior intelligence and understanding of the human condition. 'You are thinking how can you turn this situation to your own advantage, am I right? What do you need to do to survive?'

Winston was struck by Sadiq's accuracy—was he that transparent? His face must have registered surprise for Sadiq said,

'We know your thoughts, we know you better than you know yourself. Watch this, Mr Smith. Then you will understand the futility of opposing the Party.' Sadiq switched on a miniature hand-held device and the Grand Mufti filled the wallscreens. The voice and image faded and was replaced by a man wheeling his battered bag through immigration control.

His heart leaped in his chest. There he was: a scruffy thirty-three-year-old, stooped, with a bald patch. He hadn't realised how shabbily dressed he was: raggedy jeans, sloppy blue T-shirt and that old brown bomber jacket he'd bought in a Salvation Army op shop. 'Ordinary', yes that's what he was, an unremarkable, unsuspecting, ten-a-penny tourist. Even in the busy terminal he didn't warrant a second glance standing at the booth waiting for a bearded officer to return his fake passport. Winston heard the supervisor say: 'That's him: wave him through.' When the officer handed over his passport he saw the look of relief on his own face. 'Enjoy your stay, Mr Smith.' How naïve he'd been to think he'd fooled them.

The quality of their surveillance footage was extraordinary. Always watching. Always recording. Here he was pushing through a crush of people: barrows and handcarts, rows of bicycles and double-decker buses blocking the streets, the barking of stall holders, the chanting of loudspeakers, the tramping of feet. It was exhausting to watch. Here he was at the tube station staring at that old man with the filthy bowler. 'We should never have trusted the bastards!' And as Winston disappeared into the station two SIPs emerged from the shadows and marched the old man into a waiting police transit van. Winston stared at Chelsea riding the tube: there was not much to see of her shrouded figure, but he saw the tip of her finger brush the knuckles of his hand. He saw her pale English skin and the look of defiance in her sharp blue eyes. Why had he not been more suspicious of a pretty young woman traveling alone? He glanced across at Sadiq's self-satisfied face. Now Winston was standing outside a small second-hand bookshop, reading the gothic lettering over the entrance, the window draped with plastic sheeting, the sign on the door inviting him inside.

'So, do you still believe in free will, Mr Smith?'

'Yes, I do.'

'Even after all we have shown you?'

'Extremely rare, that is …' Mr Warwick was saying on the wallscreen. Winston watched himself pick up the red leather notebook and turn it over lovingly in his hands. How could they have been so certain he would buy this? Humans were never completely predictable.

Sadiq turned away from him and began strolling up and down the brightly-lit cell, tapping the air in thought with his finger. 'How do I make you understand, Mr Smith, that whatever you do, you are merely acting out our wishes.'

There was a noise in the passage and Mr Warwick entered. He was no longer wearing red braces and a stained bow tie. He was dressed in olive green fatigues with the Party's insignia of two crossed sabres over the bismillah on his epaulettes. The transformation from rumpled second-hand bookseller to this stiff paramilitary figure was astonishing. The wispy goatee had vanished along with the thick black spectacles and he snapped his heels to attention and pointed a finger at Winston: 'That is the blasphemer! That is him!'

'You asked me to read it,' Winston said.

'But you did not refuse.'

Someone had edited the surveillance tape so that it appeared as if Winston was reading the passage of his own volition: 'Between Muhammad's legs were hanging down his entrails; his heart was visible, and the dismal sack that maketh excrement of what is eaten ...'

'I didn't write those words,' he cried. 'It was Dante!'

The guard who had obviously not heard of such a person grabbed him by the throat and punched him flush in the mouth. Winston fell to the floor covering his head with his hands as the guard kicked at his head savagely with his built-up shoes.

Panting, the guard leaned against the wall.

'We love our Prophet more than we love life,' Sadiq said. 'You in the West love life more than you love God.'

'There is no God that I can see.' Winston picked himself up off the floor. His front tooth was loosened. He wobbled it with his tongue. His jaw ached. Why were they doing this to him? If it was to break him down, he was already broken but Sadiq seemed to enjoy humiliating him.

'You kuffars believe in nothing,' Sadiq said, 'and if you believe in nothing then nothing is all you are left with.'

'So you are a believer?'

'There is no God but Allah and Muhammad is his messenger,' Sadiq said. He spoke calmly and Winston was struck by the smoothness of his speech. In other circumstances he might have listened with an open mind, perhaps been swayed by his rhetoric but what they had done to Chelsea and what they had done to London meant he could never forgive. And yet he didn't hate Sadiq. He understood that he was the victor. Why continue to resist when the end result was inevitable? For decades the Islamists had preached openly in mosques of their desire to overthrow the parliamentary system, that Allah had bequeathed this country to them, that sharia law would soon rule over the land, but in the end the Party had achieved power in Britain not through the sword, but through dawah, not through acts of violence, as in other parts of the world, but through manipulating the democratic process.

'What is my future?' he said.

'You will betray the Jewess and then you will embrace Islam.'

'You want me to lead you to HER?'

'On the contrary, we want you to bring the Jewess to us.'

'I want to see Chelsea first.'

'Do you think that's wise?' Sadiq asked. 'After all, she betrayed you.'

'I don't believe that,' he said. 'She would rather die than work for you.'

Sadiq smiled again. 'This is what attracted you, was it not? Her youthful defiance, her promiscuity. What is there not to like in a pretty young woman preoccupied with sexual thoughts? Am I correct, Mr Smith?'

Winston didn't answer. Chelsea was genuine; she wasn't acting out a role. He knew her better than Sadiq did. He had slept with her, touched her skin, kissed her lips, he could tell so much from that one last kiss.

Sadiq exchanged words with Mr Warwick who stood in the doorway, his shaved head gleaming under the bright lights. Winston should have realised that he was not a bookseller by the condition of those filthy books dumped on the floor of his shop. Dead books.

'Can I get you anything, Mr Smith. A glass of water perhaps?'

Winston shook his head. He watched the cell door close behind them. Fingering his loose tooth, he blinked up at the wallscreen and there she was, her long pale limbs spread across the bed, her dark hair loose on the pillow. They had used three cameras, two of them hidden in the corners of the ceiling, a third beneath her turntable. It was embarrassing to watch his amateurish fumbling while Chelsea seemed relaxed and fluid in her nakedness, even making love she was at ease, like a natural swimmer, instinctive and intuitive, closing her eyes while he kept his open, her toes curled around his.

To think that Sadiq and others had watched Chelsea in these intimate moments. Lying in the crook of his arm thinking she was safe. Sadiq was right: he had no choice. Her fate lay in his hands. He needed to do whatever he could. Soon the Resistance would wither away and the people of Britain would know nothing other than the lies of the Islamists. How could you argue with them when their minds were set in stone? To put all your trust in a God you cannot see or hear was irrational. But this new Britain was different from anything that had existed before, and it was little men like Sadiq who were now its leaders.

# 9

The cell was designed so that wherever he sat or lay on the bed he was blinded by the lights. Even when he closed his eyes his eyelids felt inflamed. Sleep was unthinkable. The noise from the wallscreens interfered with his thoughts and yet it was impossible to look away for banks of intense fluorescent lights were recessed into the ceiling and walls in such a way that it was only by staring at the screens he could avoid looking directly into them. He tried to block out the hypnotic voice extolling the Party's economic and social achievements. The words drilled into his brain. He was losing the ability to hold on to his sanity, his head ached, he tried to imagine his daughter's face, tried to picture Sarah undressing at the foot of their bed, everyday images of a once normal life. He had no future, he existed only in the past, he dared not think of the present. It was impossible to tell how much time had elapsed since his arrest. Was it hours or days? Torture by white light was worse than darkness.

He cupped his hands over his eyes and squinted at the wallscreen between his fingers. Waves of determined-looking young men were streaming through the streets of London shouting slogans and yelling that God was greater. At first he thought they were rioting but then he realised no, they were rejoicing. The official celebrations for the anniversary of the Glorious Victory had begun. It was morning so he had been held here overnight. Three hundred and sixty-five days the Islamists had been in power. Who could have predicted it? No-one saw it coming, no-one outside the Party had anticipated them winning the general election. Why did so many people vote for the IPGB? Some claimed that religion filled a void in the lives of many young people, offering them a clean, moral and disciplined lifestyle in contrast to the materialistic excesses of the west. Others said it was because the two-party political system was broken. Voting was fragmented. The UK electoral system was vastly unrepresentative. Whatever the reason, the Islamic Party of Great Britain had secured the highest vote for any single political party in over a decade.

A massive crowd was gathering in Hyde Park. On a green-draped platform an orator from the IPGB was haranguing the crowd in preparation for the arrival of the Prime Minister. Positioned in front of the stage divided by glass partitions were rows of women shrouded in black and holding up placards denouncing the Jews and the Kuffars. There were Women for Islam and Women for Sharia. The patriotic music stopped for a BBC news flash: right wing extremists had attacked a mosque in Bradford seriously injuring two SIPs. These saboteurs, the excited newsreader was saying, held no regard for the sanctity of human life.

Then to enormous cheers and applause Prime Minister Nawaz appeared on stage. He wore a knitted white prayer cap and held his long bony hands out in front of him in a sign of humility; from side on he resembled a large bird of prey. Nawaz called on all Britons to reject the politics of hate. 'To those people who do not want to join us,' he declared, 'to those people who choose to reject our strong moral values and to resist Allah's divine laws, to those people who would resort to mockery and violence, my government's message is clear. We will hunt you down.'

A roar of approval erupted from the crowd and brought Winston to his feet. The Prime Minister had singled out HER, the Jewess, whom he blamed for the latest terror attack. Winston remembered her words: 'It will take time. And many many lives will be lost but we will prevail'. Surely this was not the extent of the mission? Surely there was more to it than this minor assault?

Prime Minister Nawaz was reading from his teleprompter. In consultation with the Grand Mufti, he declared Monday to be a national holiday. 'On this glorious day in the year 1471 of the Hijri,' the Prime Minister continued, 'the Islamic Party of Great Britain has declared by Act of Parliament that all existing laws shall be brought in conformity with the Injunctions of Islam as laid down in the Qur'an and the Sunnah, and no law shall be valid which is in opposition to such Injunctions. It is not the duty of mankind to govern, only Allah governs!

'Under my Party the social blights that have inflicted this nation for so long will be eradicated. Christians need not fear for they will be protected and allowed to practice their religion. So, too, Hindus and Buddhists. A small tax will be levied in order to maintain their houses of worship. Together, we will build a new Britain for all people. London is not just for the English. London is for all the Ummah. Only my Party can save the elderly and vulnerable from the crime and violence that used to plague our cities. Only my Party can save our young men from the drugs and alcohol that wreck their lives. Faith is the only answer. Religion is not part of life,' Prime Minister Nawaz said, raising a single finger skywards. 'Life is part of religion.'

He waited for the waves of cheering to subside. 'From this day forward,' Prime Minister Nawaz continued, 'the government I lead has declared that elections are no longer necessary. We have reached the pinnacle of the mountain, we are entering a golden age!'

An enormous roar swept through the crowd like a jet at take-off. Winston stood in the middle of the brightly-lit cell watching covered women weeping with joy and men beating their chests. He had never witnessed such jubilation. Everything the people had asked for had been delivered. No longer would there be corruption and injustice in this land, no longer would privilege and class be determined by birth, everyone would be ruled fairly by the laws laid down by Allah.

Prime Minister Nawaz paused, his words drowned out by the deafening roar. He stepped back from the microphone for a moment and bathed in the adulation of the crowd.

'Democracy,' he said, holding up a thin bony hand, 'democracy is by its very nature divisive. It contradicts Allah's law. It is merely a step on the road to spiritual awareness. This is what the history of Great Britain has been leading to. My government will forever be in the hands of Allah!'

Emotion flooded Winston's thoughts. He could not help but respond to the euphoric faces in the crowd: the immigrants, the foreigners, the Londoners crammed together in Hyde Park: old men sobbing on the shoulders of their neighbours, boys wearing green headbands bouncing up and down in their bare feet. Faith was the true answer. How easy it was to grasp that simple solution. The urge to belong, to be part of the crowd, was irresistible. Who could resist the promises the Party made? Was it not easier to put your life and your children's lives in the hands of Allah? Was this really such a bad thing?

Prime Minister Nawaz was not a natural speaker, relying heavily on his teleprompter, but it wasn't his wooden delivery that stirred the crowd into a frenzy. The Party had encouraged the association of key words with strong emotions and every time the Prime Minister mentioned Islam and Sharia, the crowd broke into rapturous applause. Bent over the podium, Nawaz reminded Winston of a thin bearded vulture. Cameras showed the hundreds of thousands of supporters gathering across the country in stadiums and parks, on heaths and moors, in mosques and schools and prison yards, in town halls and village squares and open fields, the shouting, the singing, the waving of home-made banners and black and white flags, the roaring of a squadron of jets flying low overhead, the booming of artillery down by the Thames.

'Imagine a time,' Prime Minister Nawaz went on, 'imagine a time when everyone regardless of race or country of origin works together to build a better Britain. Well that time is here! The extremists and Zionists have no vision for Britain that can sustain the dreams and ambitions of the Ummah. Only by being united under Sharia can we as a nation move forward.'

Winston squinted at the wallscreen. What could the Resistance offer to compete with such a vision? Women were free to do what they want but out of respect for Allah they were required to cover their bodies. Everyone in Britain was free to do what they want so long as they obeyed the sacred laws and scriptures.

Nawaz spoke of his government's plans to build a mighty clock tower and a giant mosque on a scale unsurpassed anywhere on earth—a sign to the world that the United Kingdom was now a major Islamic power. The PM went on to praise His Majesty, Head of the Commonwealth and Defender of the Faith. Live pictures of the old King were beamed from the balcony of Windsor Castle. Wearing a double-breasted pin-striped suit with a red carnation stuck in his lapel, the old King had put on considerable weight since his conversion and second marriage. Two steps behind him stood the royal consort wearing a traditional black veil. No-one had seen her face in public, but she was rumoured to be beautiful beyond compare. The House of Windsor and the House of Saud were now joined through blood and the prosperity of both kingdoms was assured.

The old King spoke to the crowd. He welcomed the celebrations for the first anniversary of the glorious victory of the Islamic Party of Great Britain, calling it 'a momentous event for all religions, heralding a golden age. This is a victory to unite People of the Book,' the old King said. 'Materialism is unbalanced and damaging, the Islamic civilization will help us retain an integrated and integral view of the sanctity of the world around us ...'

No-one knew what he meant, but the crowd cheered regardless. Winston watched the old King read haltingly from his prepared notes—a great faith that has enriched the lives of so many—an enriching contribution to Britain's cultural life—a model for other nations to behold.

'We should all live in peace and Islam is a proven religion of peace,' the old King declared. The young Queen stood behind him with only her coal-black eyes visible, as still as a statue.

The cameras switched to Hyde Park where the Prime Minister thanked His Majesty for his words of wisdom. Seated on the stage some distance away from Nawaz was the corpulent figure of the Grand Mufti with his thick black beard and expansive robes that flowed from his large frame. The row of imams seated behind the Grand Mufti wore beards of identical length and expansive black robes. The Grand Mufti was believed to wield supreme power inside the Party, and he and Prime Minister Nawaz carefully avoided each other on stage as if there was some deep rivalry at play.

Winston understood he was witnessing historic times, that in years to come people would look back on 2048 as a turning point in Europe just as momentous and significant as 1453.

'Thirty years ago,' the Grand Mufti continued, 'Greater London was a cesspit. Racism and Islamophobia were rampant. People had to pray in the streets for lack of mosques and were forbidden to take prayer breaks at work, but the Mu'min knew that those who obey God and his messenger will never be abandoned and that Allah will guide them to victory and so it came to pass that our Party was formed and its numbers expanded rapidly and the community spread to every town and city in Britain and claimed the allegiance of all segments of society from the House of Peers to the homeless immigrants until our numbers exceeded two million strong and we shocked the world with our victory. Today under the guidance of my Party, our men are respected and our women are now admired for their modesty. The streets have been reclaimed from the decadence and crime that has inflicted London for centuries.

'Civilisation has been restored!' the Grand Mufti said with a flourish of his arms. All praise is due to God alone. I bear witness that there is no God but Allah and I bear witness that our beloved Prophet is His Messenger. If the faithful obey the Party in this life then they will be rewarded in the next …'

Winston listened to the Grand Mufti thank members of the Council of Senior Scholars. 'We will unify the ranks of the Mujahideen,' the Grand Mufti said. 'The call for Khilafah must be raised from all corners of the Earth!

A sense of elation ran through the crowd. 'No more Elections!' they chanted, 'Democracy go to Hell!' Supporters held up placards denouncing the Jews and the enemies of Allah.

The celebrations had only begun. The Grand Mufti was due to lead a triumphal procession from Hyde Park through Piccadilly to Diversity Square where more speeches and an important announcement was to be made.

The door opened to Winston's cell and a woman entered in a black niqab covering her from head to toe. Winston assumed she was a servant for she placed a metal jug of water on the floor of the cell and kept her eyes lowered. He was hungry and thirsty and his head ached and his front tooth was loose and he had all but given up hope of ever leaving here. The bearded guard kept the cell door ajar while the woman poured water into a paper cup and when she handed it to him he saw her eyes.

He could not say what had changed in her: he sensed she was different. He took the cup and drained it in one gulp then reached out to thank her but she reared back as if in disgust.

'Don't touch me!' she said. Her voice was muffled.

'Chelsea?'

The guard watched from the doorway, ready to intervene.

'What is it?' Winston said.

Chelsea lowered her gaze.

'Is it Sadiq? Are you frightened of Sadiq?'

'Just as our men fear Allah so we must fear our husbands,' she whispered. Her speech was difficult to understand.

'I don't blame you,' he said, 'for betraying me. You did what you had to do to survive, but Sadiq is not your husband.'

'Sadiq is my protector, he's the one who showed me the true path. I was unclean,' she said. 'I fornicated with men I barely knew. I committed Zina. Allah has forbidden us doing the things that lead to it. I repented to Him and asked Him to accept my repentance.'

'And did he?' Winston said.

She blinked at him as if she sensed he was mocking her. He saw the look of fear in her eyes and smelt blood on her breath.

'I invite you to submit to Allah and you will be spared. Convert and work with us and you will be rewarded in this life and the next.'

'Let me see your face,' he said. He feared they had done something terrible to her.

'The return of the veil is a great achievement for women,' she said. 'We can walk the streets unmolested. It liberates us from the tyranny of fashion. The Party protects us from ourselves and from our desires. Our task is not to distract the eyes of our men, but to serve them and to serve Allah.

'Repent,' she said, 'repent your sins, Winston.'

'What sins?'

'Fornication between a man and an unmarried woman is forbidden.'

He wanted to shake some sense into her. He glanced over at the guard who was eyeing her closely. Of course, every word of hers was being recorded. Surely this was a test to ensure Chelsea had learned the proper principles. Or was she trying to relay a warning? What a fine actor she was, how convincing.

'The Party is a champion of women's rights,' Chelsea said. 'We have never been so free as when we serve Allah.'

She was talking faster and faster, the words tumbling from her mouth as if she had to get them out. There was nothing he could say in reply. It was hard enough understanding what she was saying through that coarse black cloth. What worried him was the agitated look in her eyes.

'We don't realise how forgiving and wonderful the Party is, how empowering it is to know that He is watching over us, that everything we do and say and think is known to Him.'

The lights in the cell gave him a migraine. He had a ringing in his ears. It was impossible to listen to this babble any longer. She looked up at him and said softly so the guard couldn't hear: 'I forgive you, Winston.'

'I forgive you too.' There was a flicker in her blue eyes, a momentary spark of life and then it was gone. 'Let me see your face,' he said, 'let me see your face one last time …'

Chelsea lifted her veil slowly.

'What have they done to you?' he said.

'I was unclean,' she said, 'my mind and body were infected with impurities. The poison had entered my bloodstream causing immorality. I feel cleansed now, I no longer have sinful urges.'

Her mouth had collapsed: the lips that he had kissed were sunk into her gums. They had pulled all her teeth. She covered her face with her veil and turned away. She said something more that he didn't catch as the guard approached.

Without thinking he ran at the guard, knocking him to the floor and pounding at his face with his fists. Immediately there was a stampede of boots in the corridor and something heavy smacked into the back of his head. He rolled onto the concrete floor of the cell where he remained without moving.

When he came to, his thoughts were scattered and he had to gather them one by one: the blinding lights, the white-walled cell, the blathering wallscreen. Pain split the rear of his skull and he couldn't feel his hands tethered behind his back. Chelsea was gone and the door to the cell was sealed. Drops of blood gleamed on the floor and he lay face down, plastic cables cutting into his wrists. He stared at a chip of ceramic tile on the floor. It looked like a tooth. He probed the fresh hole inside his mouth with his tongue. The lights dimmed and Sadiq entered, his silvery hair slicked back, dark circles under his eyes.

'Are you comfortable, Mr Smith? Restraints not too tight?'

He didn't answer.

'What did you hope to achieve by such foolishness? Nobody cares if you live or die. I am your only friend in the world. Without me you are nothing.'

He struggled to sit up. 'Why do you hate us?' he said.

'We don't hate you,' Sadiq said. 'We have superseded you. We played by your rules and we won. Surely there can be no argument with that?'

Winston looked up at him. How do you argue with someone more intelligent than you when you know they are wrong?

'We are not in England to integrate,' Sadiq said. 'We are here to dominate. We will conquer Europe and then we will conquer North America.' Sadiq smiled again. 'You are thinking to yourself why then is he so polite? Because I value good manners, that's why. I value courtesy and respect for others. There is no excuse for rudeness.'

'You disfigured her,' he said.

'Don't exaggerate, Mr Smith. The job of women is to have babies and care for the home—not to engage in immoral sexual behaviour. Women must know their place. I gain no pleasure from punishing those women who transgress but we must safeguard the morality of Britain. You think we are cruel, but discipline is essential. Chelsea will be provided with a set of dentures and a suitable husband. She has been promised already to someone who will respect her properly. Unless you wish to marry her yourself, that is?'

Winston hesitated.

'I thought not. You must know that she betrayed you. You should have seen how willingly she confessed. She said you were old and unattractive, those were her words, she said that she only slept with you out of pity. Don't try to romanticise your feelings, Mr Smith. This was no great love affair, there was no commitment on your behalf, if so you would have protected that vulnerable young woman; instead you used her to satisfy your carnal desires. It was disgusting to watch.'

'It wasn't like that,' he said.

'This is the problem with sexual promiscuity. It reduces us to the level of animals. Look at you, trussed like a turkey.'

'Can you untie me?' he said.

'Actions have consequences, Mr Smith. That is a lesson you must learn. Take your punishment and I'll return shortly.'

Sadiq strode from the white-walled cell, the metal caps on his shoes tapping lightly on the concrete. Three guards entered, one wielding an expandable rubber truncheon. He recognised the guard he had assaulted: his cheekbone was puffed and discoloured. Instinctively he curled into a ball on the floor, tucking his chin into his chest. The first blow drove everything else from his mind, a terrible agonising pain that made him scream. After the second blow, he begged them to stop. Writhing on the floor in pain, nothing else mattered except this point in time. He screwed up his eyes, clenching his teeth as the truncheon struck the soles of his feet. Boots thudded into the base of his spine, and under his ribs. The guards used only their boots and a truncheon with the steel rod inside. Urine dribbled down his legs. How long they beat him he did not know; all sense of time stopped. The guards laughed at the strings of snot and mucus dangling off his chin. He could only wriggle and writhe and squeal, trapped like an animal. And then abruptly the beating stopped.

Someone cut the cable ties on his wrists but he could not move his arms. He had lost all sensation in his hands and feet. It was agony to hold up his head. When he tried to sit up he toppled over so he lay on the floor of the cell, mouth open, listening to the reassuring sound of his own heavy breathing. Thankfully the wallscreen was muted but he could see a procession of men moving through Hyde Park. He took refuge in thoughts of his childhood, trying to regain some feeling in his fingers. Pain spread through every part of his body. All his resistance was gone. He sensed rather than heard Sadiq enter the cell. He stared at the tiny perforations in his polished brogues.

'So, Mr Smith,' Sadiq said. 'You admit you are a terrorist?'

'Yes, I do,' Winston said.

'Who planned to murder innocent Muslims?'

'Yes,' he said.

'Good.' Sadiq smiled pleasantly. 'Now we know the full extent of your crimes. Your only choice is to submit to the will of Allah.'

'I understand,' he said. He was to betray the Jewess. Bring her to them. He had no doubts about his situation, there was no one to rescue him, no-one to intervene, no-one to mourn his passing once he was gone. The only path was to obey. Perhaps they were right, perhaps there was no such thing as free will. Perhaps the freedoms everyone imagined in the West were only illusions.

'You belong to us now,' Sadiq said.

Winston wriggled his toes; the soles of his feet, the backs of his arms and his ribs were numb. He tried again to sit up but he could not push himself off the floor. How could they be certain he would betray HER?

'Because we know you Mr Smith,' Sadiq said, reading his thoughts.

'We know your motivations, and, most importantly, we know your fears.'

'What happens to me now?'

'You are free to go.' Sadiq gestured towards the door.

It was a trap. The moment he walked out of his cell the guards would set upon him again with their truncheons and boots. He could not withstand another beating. He was terribly afraid. His hands shook uncontrollably, he tried not to burst into tears. He stammered out his refusal.

'So, you want to stay here?' Sadiq said. He seemed to find this amusing. 'I'm afraid you have work to do, Mr Smith.' Sadiq held out his shoes. They had been re-soled and re-heeled. 'The crimes you have committed deserve serious punishment but you have one last opportunity to prove yourself.'

An image floated into Winston's mind of Sarah and he clung to it desperately. She was unwavering in her determination. He tried to show some dignity and pulled himself up onto the bed. Every muscle in his arms ached and he felt a penetrating pain behind his ribs as if he had ruptured a kidney. Bending to lace up his shoes made him wince out loud. It was as if his entire body had been hammered out of shape.

'You have until nightfall,' Sadiq explained. 'My men will drop you near Covent Garden.'

If they knew about the blind man why did they need him? Why not find HER themselves?

'There's more than one way to trap a Jewish rat,' Sadiq said with a smile.

'What about Chelsea?'

'Her happiness depends on your co-operation. In time she will forget about you, she will dedicate herself to serving her husband, she may even have children—who knows if she is capable given her wanton immorality?'

He hated Sadiq with such a fury but he could not let his face betray him. Sadiq was watching him closely. 'Remember, Mr Smith. You have no choice in anything you do.' And he walked off leaving the cell door open.

For some time he huddled on the edge of the bed, waiting for the guards to re-appear. All he could think of was his own pain. It suffocated his ability to focus. Maybe they had forgotten about him. He managed to stand but found he could only shuffle forward like a broken old man. It was hard to fathom why they were letting him go. It didn't make sense. If they knew about the tunnels why then did they need him to betray HER? He shuffled out into the corridor. A young man wearing the uniform of the militias was waiting by the lift. He greeted him with recognition. It was Mafid. His top lip sprouted strands of uneven dark hair.

'What are you doing here?' he asked.

'Carrying out the will of God,' Mafid said.

Winston wanted to respond, but nothing came to mind. He pointed to the cursive lettering running across Mafid's headband and said, 'How long have you been working for the IIS?'

Mafid said nothing. When the doors opened he gripped Winston's arm and led him forcefully out through the foyer and into the street. A man was washing his dirty feet with bottled water over the gutter. People hurried past as if they were late for some important event.

He glanced up at the clock and over at the swollen brown Thames. He did not know how long he had been held in there, 12, 14 hours at most, but he was not the same man who had entered this building the night before. Walking was difficult; his feet refused to go where he willed them. He didn't understand what game Sadiq was playing. All the trouble the IIS had gone to from the moment he'd landed in London, using Chelsea as bait, monitoring his every movement with the intention of him leading them to HER. So why not pick him up earlier? Why waste all this time and resources? Was he their only asset or was the Resistance compromised from within? He pictured O'Connell in Sydney; he could not believe the big Irishman had betrayed them. The other possibility was that he had talked in his sleep; he was untrained and unskilled, writing down his forbidden thoughts in a second-hand notebook only demonstrated his ineptitude. If only he hadn't been so stupid. And yet the Resistance had seen something in him of value.

A black saloon awaited on the far side of the road, the same shiny German vehicle that had brought him here. He heard the muezzin's call to prayer in the distance. Not ten metres away from the rear of the car he saw Chelsea. He couldn't be sure it was her and yet he was convinced it was. Her height and stance were instantly familiar even shrouded in that black niqab. She walked with head bowed, penitent, not looking back. Did she realise he was standing here? She was walking two steps behind a tall man wearing a turban, grey-bearded, and ancient enough to be her grandfather. He was overwhelmed by a desire to call out her name, yell something across the crowded street that would make her stop and turn and acknowledge his existence. Above all, he wanted her recognition. He wanted her to know that he was thinking of her, that he would always think of her…

Mafid tightened his grip as if he sensed Winston was about to dash across the traffic but his legs were incapable of dashing anywhere. The soles of his feet were too sore. When he looked up she was gone, swallowed up by the crowds heading for the celebrations. Mafid guided him across to the waiting car with its black tinted windows and assisted him into the back seat. Winston thanked him. 'We are the best of Allah's creations,' Mafid said, without any sense of irony.

The door slammed and he turned his head to steal a glance out the rear window. From the river-side a closed-circuit camera swivelled on its metal arm as if it were following him. He stared up at the blinking red eye. There was no escape. Sadiq was right. It was too late. The end was inevitable.

# 10

He picked his way through Covent Garden searching for the blind man. It was past midday and he was late. Groups of armed militia were handing out sweets to ragged children. It was impossible to move faster than a shuffle through the swelling crowd. No-one paid any attention to him; he stared into the faces of pilgrims and travellers who had crossed the channel, many of them carrying their meagre possessions in salvaged shopping bags: Prada, Mulberry, Giorgio, Tiffany. Young men were leaping about like frogs. The rule of God was the only rule! Sharia was the only law!

Winston was overwhelmed by waves of cheering and clapping. All further resistance was futile. If he wanted to continue living he had to betray HER. Whatever mission the Resistance had planned for him was now compromised. He threw up his hands and cried, 'Obey the Party! Obey the Messenger!' Strangers smiled and a furry old man clapped his back saying, 'Peace be upon those who follow the true path.'

He wished he had his notebook, he wished he could write down his thoughts but the time for thinking was past. He didn't believe in God but there was a voice in his head spurring him on, it was not Sarah's or Tess's or Chelsea's or even HER's—it was a female voice from within. Make use of the time you have left, the voice said. Don't be afraid. What did that mean? Had he suffered a brain injury from the repeated blows to his head? It was more likely a hallucination, but he could hear the voice clearly, deep inside his skull, speaking to him softly, guiding him through the mass of people blocking the northern side of the square. He remembered O'Connnell's words, 'Look for the light within, it will guide you through the darkness'.

Even if it was a delusion the voice gave him strength; he was not alone in the world and he had someone to converse with. His lips moved as he hobbled through the crowd. People gave him strange looks now, staring at his bruised and battered face and shifted aside to allow him through. What a mess he must appear, muttering away to himself. Another demented soul loose on the streets of London. They weren't to know what choices had led him to this moment. It didn't matter, the voice said, soon enough you'll be free. He breathed in the sooty air, grateful to still be alive. He heard the cacophony of buses and ratchets and horns. All his senses were enhanced. He gazed into the joyous faces of strangers. Wouldn't it be wonderful if all the answers for humanity were written down in one little book and if you followed its instructions to the letter you would be rewarded in the afterlife. What did you have to lose? The Party promised that people's lives and the lives of their children would be transformed. Unwavering obedience is all they asked for. Was that too high a price to pay?

A girl of no more than fourteen pushed across his path pulling the hand of a much younger girl. From their similar flaxen hair he assumed they were sisters. They both wore mascara and smeared lipstick and their dresses were far too short. 'Excuse me, mister … which way t'it feast? Me and er's right ungry.'

Winston said, 'It's not safe to get around like that.'

'Like wot?' The girl scowled and rubbed her dirty face.

'Cover your hair and your arms and ankles.'

'It's bleedin hot,' the girl said. 'We been on the road for days.'

'Are you from the north?' he said.

‘Aye, they told us there were feasting here all weekend, s’much food as you can carry.’

He dug in his pockets and gave her a ten-pound coin. ‘Take this, find something to eat and go home. It’s not safe for you in London.’

‘Are you French, mister? The way you speak ain’t half funny.’ Her little sister looked at him with big brown eyes like a calf.

‘Stay off the streets and don’t get into any unlicensed minicabs,’ he warned. The girl snatched the money then pulled her safety scarf up over her hair and pulled down the sleeves of her thin cardigan. She didn’t thank him and, dragging her sister behind her like a rag doll, she melted into the crowd.

He reached the tube station but the blind man was not in his usual spot selling shoelaces and razor blades. Maybe the Resistance had learned of his arrest. Surely, they had eyes on the street. For the hundredth time, he asked himself why the Resistance had chosen him. It was not for his knowledge of history for no-one valued the past anymore: the past was something to be ashamed of, rather than celebrated. Although the government had dismissed fifty thousand public employees; in all of Britain there were possibly no more than a few thousand active members of the Resistance, the mules and recruiters who worked behind the scenes, the planners and fighters. Winston knew the Party’s goal was Shakespeare. If they cut off her head, the Resistance would rot and yet he had no choice but to betray her. He could not endure another beating.

He looked up at the clock above Covent Garden tube station, its hands had been removed and its face was blank. The voice in his head told him to remain outside the station. If he was so vital to their mission surely the blind man would find him. There was nothing else he could do. He stared at the clock with no hands. Time had run out. He thought of those pale freckled sisters from the north and wondered how long they would survive.

He had never seen so many people clogging the streets. Penned together like cattle, they streamed south for the feasting and festivities. Beads of sweat mingled with the blood in his beard. He needed to piss and did so up against the station's tiled wall. Nobody seemed to care. The temptation to lie down on the road was overwhelming. The female voice inside his head urged him to stay awake, to keep going, and then iron fingers gripped his arm and a voice said,

'You're late!'

The blind man was wearing an embroidered skull-cap and long white robe but it was the plastic contraption wrapped around his eyes that caught his attention. 'Take off your shoes.'

'Why?'

'Do it,' the blind man said.

Winston removed his shoes and the blind man threw them into the gutter. Within moments they were scavenged by two barefoot boys pushing a rickety cart. The blind man handed him a pair of cheap sandals and a set of thick black glasses with wires. The sandals were too small and the glasses plunged the daylight into darkness. 'I can't see!' he said.

'Take my arm,' the blind man said. 'Follow my instructions. If anyone stops us we're two blind men returning home.'

Winston understood but questioned why his own vision needed to be impaired. At best, he could make out shapes and outlines but no colours: some kind of electronic chip was embedded in the frames for they gave off a warning beep whenever he approached an obstacle. The leather sandals pinched his feet. No one paid him any attention despite the fact they were heading in the opposite direction to everyone else, skirting the edges of office buildings. A pair of SIPs eyed them in passing with a sort of guarded curiosity but they didn't stop or demand identification. Winston had no idea where they were going, winding through narrow cobbled streets, past dark arched doorways that smelled of leaking sewage. There were no trees anywhere just iron lace and blackened limestone, washing dripping from balconies. Rats exploded from an open drain in front of them and he heard their excited squealing.

After a distance, he became accustomed to the e-glasses and his sense of smell began to grow stronger, his hearing more acute. He clung to the blind man's sinewy arm, obeying his instructions to turn right here and veer left there. It was as if the blind man carried a map of London inside his head. All Winston knew was that they were somewhere south east of the river, heading into the poorer parishes. They passed a barefoot beggar dragging a mattress encased in clear plastic. Here the streets were emptied of traffic. How old this blind man was Winston could only guess, he wanted to ask if he was ex-military but knew the Resistance discouraged personal questions. He didn't even know his name. Whoever he was he was stronger and fitter and when Winston began to tire the blind man dragged him along with the determination of a mule. 'How much further?' he called. The sandals hurt, his mouth hung open; he felt mauled and eaten up, his spirit broken.

Way off to the west came a blast louder than thunder and then the booming roaring sound of a 21-gun salute. Fireworks lit the sky and a formation of jets flew low overhead. The official celebrations for the introduction of Sharia law were in full swing.

The blind man stopped and patted him down, asked if he owned a watch. Winston shook his head and gave the blind man back his e-glasses. The grey London sky was covered in a patina of green and the air tasted of copper.

'We must be careful,' the blind man said. 'Their eyes and ears are everywhere.'

He stared at the tiny purple veins on the blind man's nose and the straggly white whiskers on his chin. 'My shoes,' he said, breathing heavily, 'was there something in those shoes?' The blind man didn't answer. They were standing outside a small gothic church tucked between two monstrous apartment buildings. Its stone exterior had fallen into disrepair and the stained glass on the west side had been vandalized. 'What church is this?'

'The Church of the Saviour,' the blind man said. 'For over a thousand years Christians have worshipped here.' He tapped three times on the heavy wooden door. It opened with a rough, grinding noise and a tall Jamaican-looking man with hair bee-hived and skewered on top of his head waved them inside and then bolted the door behind them with a clank of iron.

The church smelled of damp and mildew as if it had been shut up for years. Just inside the entrance was a monument to those who had died in the Great War. A simple carved pulpit stood on a wooden platform and behind it was a white marble cartouche complete with skulls and an hourglass. As he entered the church Winston stopped to look at the canopied pews on either side of the nave. He wasn't religious but this small interior with its medieval bell tower and dark wooden furnishings gave him a sense of calm. He wanted to rest awhile on a pew and gather his strength, but the blind man hurried him towards the south-east corner of the church where a set of narrow stone stairs led down through an arched tunnel to a large underground chamber.

Jammed inside were at least a hundred or so people standing shoulder to shoulder, and in the confined space their hushed voices hummed like bees. He stared at their faces: men and women of all races and colours. Most of the women wore headscarves. There were far more women than men present. None of them were familiar but he knew without being told that he was looking at the core of the Resistance. What a poor physical specimen he was in comparison.

Moisture dripped down the stone walls. When he stretched on his toes to see further, Winston bumped his head against a brick arch. They were in some sort of cavern that must have been an air raid shelter in

WWII. He felt a sense of belonging, the unspoken camaraderie that exists between strangers drawn together by common cause. For the first time since he'd landed in London he had found his tribe. Most likely he would never set eyes on any of these people again and somehow that made this moment more potent. It was risky to gather so many members of the Resistance in one confined space. No matter the precautions each of them took in entering this church, there was always someone spying for the Islamists, their cameras and drones and informers ever vigilant. London's police could not be trusted for their senior officers had long been politicized and were only concerned with furthering their own careers. The humming of voices intensified and an uneasy energy ran through the crowd. Winston could sense it, the shared realisation that they were trapped down here and that any moment they might be raided and arrested.

He wanted to ask the three women of varying ages beside him what was going on: one was young, one was older than her, and one was older than both of them, but despite the friendliness of their smiles he understood that asking questions was discouraged. It was at least five degrees warmer in here with so many bodies crammed together and the faces of the three women were flushed with heat. He felt an arm move him aside and a voice said, 'Thanks, Chief'. Two large security men were clearing a path through the crowd and then the humming ceased and a silence descended over the cavern. Someone was being assisted up onto the raised wooden platform by the far wall.

It was HER, the one they called Shakespeare, the one the media described as The Queen of Hate.

A ripple of applause swept through the crowd but she suppressed it with a wave of her hand. Everyone stared at her in silence. Winston felt they were thinking the same thing he was thinking—how ill she looked, how drained. Her face, her thinning hair, the way she held her head. Under her white blouse, the skin hung loosely from her arms and neck. She coughed repeatedly and cleared her throat. Had she contracted some bacterial infection from residing underground? Half of London's boroughs now suffered high rates of drug-resistant TB. A guard brought her a drink of water and she sipped at it, nodding to indicate she was fine, but then the coughing worsened. Whatever was wrong with her she needed to be treated in a hospital.

On the walls hung black and white photographs from the blitz: Londoners curled up asleep in street clothes; hats and coats hooked on nails; a helmeted fire warden stepping between tangled bodies. The members of the Resistance were their descendants and Winston was proud to stand among them. He wished he had been stronger, wished he had their courage; he was never a fighter, merely a history teacher. People didn't understand how important that job was, that without history they were nothing, that as a people they did not exist.

He stared at these old framed photos on the walls; no-one else seemed to pay them any mind. Everyone was waiting for Shakespeare to announce why she had summoned them. No-one knew her real name; even the Council of 12 did not know each other's birth names. In the end it did not matter what you were called. Shakespeare was not so much a woman as an idea.

When she had finished coughing, she stepped forward to address the crowd without a script or a microphone. 'Men and women of the Resistance,' she began. 'One hundred years ago our ancestors defeated the Nazis and today the enemy we face is larger and more entrenched in our cities. This is a different kind of war but make no mistake this is a war that will determine whether we survive on our feet or bend our knees in submission. The enemy is fanatical but we have something they do not have, we have control of our own destinies. There is no other life, only this one. There is no other life, only this one!'

'There is no other life, only this one!' The chant spread through the cavern. In a corner Marlon Jones with his braided hair was pumping the air with a fist. So, he *was* part of the Resistance.

'What we in Europe face today,' she said, 'is a war waged against the democratic world. This is a war for the future of our civilization. Let us speak the truth here. The threat today comes not from outside, but from those who have already burrowed their way inside our borders.

'Some say this is a hundred years war. Well, they are wrong. This is a thousand years war. We are fighting the last of the great totalitarian ideologies. All totalitarian ideologies rely on unquestioning obedience. Control of every aspect of human existence is their intention. We defeated Communism and we defeated Fascism. Now we must defeat a far more insidious ideology because the Islamists mask their intentions behind the guise of a religion.

'Resistance, no matter the means, is our legitimate right. Resist those who would betray the land in which your ancestors are buried. Resist those who would dictate what you should say and what you should think. Resist them while you still can. For they are the darkness and we are the light.

'If your government no longer represents your culture, then it no longer represents you. If your government does not stand up for your rights and freedoms then it no longer stands for you. We have built a great civilisation over two millennia and it is up to us to preserve it. This is your land, my brothers and sisters, and we do not submit to Sharia.

'I have summoned you here for a reason, to let you know that my time amongst you is limited. Do not feel sorry for me, for you have a far more important task at hand, particularly the brave women of Britain. For the future of our children rests on your shoulders. If you will not take up this fight then who will? Stand up and oppose their lies and ignorance. Stand up and speak out for what you believe.'

For such a tiny misshapen woman, she was an electrifying speaker. Another woman next to Winston raised a hand to speak. She was pencil-thin with a long, freckled face and her cheeks were pierced with silver pins. 'Marseilles is gone!' she said. 'Carcassone and Aix en Provence too.'

'What news of Spain?'

A gaunt middle-aged man with scarred facial features called from the far side of the cavern: 'Bad news, ma'am. The Galicians hold the north but in the south Cordoba has fallen and in Granada the bells are silenced once more. The cry of the adhan can be heard across the olive fields.'

Other fighters shared first-hand reports of their own cities from Palermo to Malmö. Pockets of resistance fought on in the Netherlands; the Poles, Czechs and Slovakians held firm, the Hungarians too. Sweden and Belgium were overrun. Much of France and southern Italy was already lost.

Winston looked around at the faces of these men and women in the crowd. The Resistance was the last line of defence. A gloomy silence descended over the cavern. Water trickled down the eroded brick walls which had lost much of their lime mortar. In some places, the brick face had begun to flake off, a sign that the Thames was getting in. Fist-size cracks radiated from the corners of this underground chamber that had once been a church crypt, then an air-raid shelter and later a venue for London's jazz and blues bands. Now it was abandoned and fallen into disrepair, dangerously unstable. If anything should happen down here, they were trapped.

While he listened, Winston shifted his weight from leg to leg. The soles of his feet ached, his arms and ribs. How could he betray HER and live with his conscience? How could he betray everything he believed? His friends said he'd changed after he met Sarah, but it was the world that had changed. He remembered watching the triple attacks on television. Operation Trojan Horse. After Sarah's death, all their conversations and interactions took on added significance as if his life, on reflection, had a purpose, but he had been unable to see it at the time.

The Islamists are the main source of oppression for women in the world, Sarah had said. It baffled her why so many of her closest friends failed to see this. What she would have given to be standing beside him now in this crowded London cavern, and yet in a strange way she was. After her passing, Sarah became part of him in a way that she hadn't been when she was alive. It was something he never mentioned to anyone, but her death had transformed his life.

Shakespeare smiled in his direction and he waved back. Others turned their heads to sneak a glance at him as if they should know who he was. He was nothing, a nobody, but for an instant he felt an enormous sense of pride that the Head of the European Resistance had acknowledged him in public. If only things were different. Standing on that platform adjusting her black-framed glasses on the end of her nose, she seemed frail and vulnerable. Not the formidable adversary the Party feared. It was her intellect, her ability to deride their dogmas and challenge their falsehoods that infuriated them. Rather than debate her, they wanted to silence her.

She coughed into her handkerchief and said, 'I have come among you on this day, not for my pleasure nor my good health, poor as it is, but being resolved, in the midst of this fight, to lay down my life for my country and my people. Every politician in Britain has betrayed us. They have sold out our principles and our freedoms. They sneer at our traditions while our media lie to us. We have emasculated our own culture, for what? For an ideology with a history of intolerance and misogyny. We are the European Resistance and our time has come. Let the Islamists fear *us*! Let *them* tremble when they hear *our* name. We shall kill *them* wherever they flee. We shall target their leaders and those traitors who have betrayed us. We must defend our land.'

Shakespeare covered her mouth and coughed harshly. 'Many of you have risked your lives to be here today,' she continued after a pause, 'and

I am grateful for your courage. No matter what happens we must not accept defeat. There is too much at stake.'

Applause broke out in the cavern and grew louder until everyone, including Winston, was clapping wildly. Even in the midst of his betrayal he admired her defiance. She was not faking her emotions; she was genuine. Here was a leader you could put your faith in.

Shakespeare removed her thick-lensed glasses and looked straight at him. 'My sisters and brothers,' she said, 'the Resistance has been infiltrated. One of you here today will betray me.'

A howl of protest rose from the front sections of the crowd; the three women standing beside him shook their heads in dismay.

'There is a traitor among us. Step forward if you have the courage!'

Winston didn't move. No-one did. She was speaking to him as if she could read his thoughts. He was sure of it.

'Which one of you is my Judas?'

It was Winston of course—she knew it was him—she knew he had betrayed her, betrayed his deepest beliefs. He had no choice. They'd beaten him to the edge of death. He glanced around at the shadowy faces in the dimly-lit cavern. Once Shakespeare was dead what would happen to all these other fighters? Most likely they would be rounded up, interrogated and incarcerated. For the young women, their lives would never be the same.

People were murmuring with disquiet. Shakespeare held up a hand and a silence fell over the cavern. 'We shall soon have a great victory,' she said. 'Arrangements are being made. Our mission is nearing completion. No-one knows about this meeting today. All communication was done by word of mouth. So, we are safe here for the moment, but when you leave, leave quietly, and in pairs. May your God go with you.'

People began shuffling in single file towards the narrow staircase that wound its way up to the small medieval church. Surely one of them knew he had been arrested, surely the Resistance had eyes and ears on the street? And yet if they knew of his betrayal, why bring him here, why expose all these other fighters to danger? It didn't make sense. Part of him wanted to confess, to beg for forgiveness. If he explained to Shakespeare about the beating, would she understand? From the look she'd given him he was convinced she knew what he'd done and yet instead of unmasking him she'd kept silent. Why?

Marlon was talking to a bald man at the foot of the stairs. Only a few members of the Resistance now remained in the cavern. The rest had flowed up and out through the north door. Winston greeted the tour guide with enthusiasm. 'Hey Marlon,' he said, staring at his Budget Decker badge. 'Remember me?'

Marlon's eyes were red and he rubbed at them with irritation. The collar of his workman's shirt was grimy and he was wearing the same faded suit, or one just like it, held together with safety pins, and a pair of sneakers.

'I was on your bus the other day.'

'This is the history teacher I told you about,' Marlon said to the bald man whom he introduced simply as The Greek.

Winston went to shake The Greek's hand then saw the man was missing three fingers and a chunk of his thumb. He had the sad, unhappy look of an intellectual. Winston mumbled an apology, trying not to stare at the man's stump. From the Greek's silence he realized he'd intruded on some private conversation. He said to Marlon, 'You told me there was another Winston Smith. What happened to him?'

Marlon didn't look at him directly. 'I tried to warn you.'

'Warn me what?'

'St Martin-in-the Fields is where the IIS picked him up.'

'Where is he now?'

'The authorities say he died of a heart attack, but his family claim that he was tortured,' Marlon said.

'I thought you were working for the Party,' Winston said.

‘They tried to recruit me, they try to recruit everyone,’ Marlon said. ‘I was an eye surgeon, they promised to reinstate me if I helped them—but I refused. What happened to your face?’

Winston touched his battered cheekbone. He had forgotten what a mess he must appear and mumbled something about a car accident. It wasn’t convincing. Surely Marlon suspected that he was the Judas, but he didn’t question him further. It was as if Marlon and the Greek knew he was lying but they were in on the deception.

The Greek said, ‘I support the Islamists at first, I welcome them as brothers. I thought they are grateful, but they turn on me and arrest me.’

‘What for?’ Winston said.

The Greek carried a medical bag in his left hand and his rimless oval glasses gave him a bookish look. ‘They threaten me that my wife and son will wear black because I don’t shut my mouth. I tell them that I only write down what I see but they say they will shut me up for good.’

‘Are you a journalist?’

‘An anarchist,’ the Greek said.

‘What kind of anarchist?’ He felt a hand grip his elbow from behind and turned to see the blind man. ‘Shakespeare wants to see you,’ he whispered.

He wanted to ask what for, but he knew what for. He followed the blind man across the floor of the cavern past the old black and white photos of Britons at war and a row of wooden crosses bearing the names, he read, of the 1st Battalion Welsh Guards Killed in Action in 1917. He had the sense that he was sleepwalking through history. The Resistance was never going to win. It was too late to undo the damage that had been done.

The blind man glided up the stairs, light-footed in his canvas slip-ons. At the top Winston followed him through the arched tunnel to the church’s modest interior with its barrel-vaulted roof and bell turret.

He stopped to rest on a pew, staring at a plaster statue of the Virgin Mary, which had lost its nose. Whatever punishment the Resistance had in store for him he could not suffer any more pain. He was tired and hungry and his bones ached.

The blind man turned back and stood over him like a priest in his white robe and cap. 'Where were you last night?' he said.

'I spent the night with a woman.'

'The Intelligence Services know of our mission,' the blind man said. 'There is a traitor in our midst.'

'What is our mission?'

'You'll find out.'

Winston looked up at the medieval belfry; the church was small and slots were set in the stone walls at an angle. At the north end, there was an additional wing, not part of the original structure, and the massive wooden door that led to it would have at one time been the external door. He had never seen a door to equal it. It must have been a thousand years old, studded with rose-head nails and held together by blackened iron straps.

'That's the devil's door.' The blind man pointed. 'All these old churches had one. It was left open during baptism to let evil spirits out.'

Now it stood slightly ajar and Winston could hear female voices coming from inside.

'Shakespeare is meeting with the Council of 12,' the blind man said. 'Wait here until you are called.' And he hurried off between the blocks of pews.

From the outside, he might have passed this old iron church without giving it a second thought, but inside it was quiet and filled with light from its cracked and broken windows. He traced a finger over the faded initials carved into his pew, thinking of all the people, heads bowed, who had prayed here, generation upon generation, and now the bronze alloy bells had been ripped from their wooden frame, and there was nothing left of value to ransack or steal. The air had a closed-in dank smell. He had made up his mind to confess. Throw himself on HER mercy. He had no choice. He had been kicked and bashed and beaten, had his front tooth knocked out, but he did not wish to die. He was terribly afraid of death. Once the Resistance learned of his betrayal he did not expect to live long. Surely, they would execute him and yet he had committed no crime. All he had done was agree under duress to bring Shakespeare to them. That's what baffled him. If the Intelligence Services had wanted him to lead them to Shakespeare why not follow him from Heathrow? Sadiq knew everything already, he knew about the mission, so why go to all the bother of planting that notebook and arranging his brief relationship with Chelsea?

For someone so unimportant they had gone to a lot of trouble to steer him around like a goat.

The oak door opened with a groan and he caught a glimpse of women seated at a long table—was this the Council of 12? And then out came Shakespeare flanked by security. At first glance, she seemed so small and shrunken, but as she approached, he sensed the aura surrounding her. She waved her two huge bodyguards away and leaned over and kissed him on both cheeks. She sat down in the pew across the aisle.

'Do you believe in the Resistance, Winston?'

'Yes,' he said.

'And you realise how important this fight is not just for Britain, but for all of Europe?'

'Yes, I do.'

She held his gaze for a moment, observing him through her large black-framed glasses. Her voice when she spoke was soft in tone: 'They asked you to betray me, didn't they?'

He glanced at her two scarred bodyguards standing out of earshot. There was no point lying. 'Yes,' he said.

'We know what the IIS did to that young woman. I'm glad you had the courage to tell me the truth.'

Shakespeare, the Jewess, HER. None of these pseudonyms did her justice. He wished he knew her real name, wished he'd gotten to know this woman while Sarah was still alive. Until you have been beaten half to death lying on the concrete floor of a stinking prison cell, you don't know how desperate you are to survive.

She reached over and laid her hand on his wrist. 'We don't have much time left, Winston. We must act swiftly.'

'Tell me,' he said, 'what is our mission?'

She didn't take her eyes off him: 'We're going to cut off the head of the snake.'

# 11

Shakespeare turned away, overcome with a paroxysm of coughing. After some time, she stopped coughing and turned to face him, her eyes filled with water, and dabbed at the corners of her mouth. Her scrunched-up handkerchief was spotted with blood. 'Are you okay?' he said.

'It'll pass,' she said. Her voice sounded raspy like a chain smoker's and she studied him closely through her oversized glasses. She was a plain-looking woman of late middle age but there was something about her, a presence, a calmness, that put him at ease. Her bodyguards had disappeared through the north door leaving them alone in this small medieval church with its dark wood and dank air.

He gestured around him. 'Who built this place?'

'It was a Saxon church originally, a priory and a convent. It was rebuilt after the Great Fire of 1212, then damaged in an earthquake and partly destroyed in the blitz.'

From his seat Winston looked up at the barrel-vaulted roof with its exposed struts and saw something fluttering on the uppermost ledge. It was a bird, a baby starling, thrashing its wings and twisting its body to free itself from a large spider's web. For such a small bird it put up a mighty struggle flapping about on the ledge and stirring up motes of dust, then after a rest trying again, pecking desperately at the sticky threads that entangled its feathers. Somehow the fledgling wrenched its wings free of the web and flew up to the roof turning and wheeling in flight.

'That's the first bird I've seen in London!' he said. 'It must have got in through that window.' He was glad Shakespeare didn't try to draw some parable from the starling's plight. Instead she told him that there used to be other birds nesting up there but the rats had eaten their eggs. Droppings mixed with uneven layers of dust coated the flagstone floor and shafts of light poured in through the stained-glass windows. He tried not to stare into the light. 'So why do they call you Shakespeare?'

'In another life I was a Professor of English Literature,' she said. 'A long time ago now.'

'Your speech in the cavern, it reminded me of this Moroccan woman who was executed in Tangier. My wife kept her poster in our study.'

'Sol Hachuel!' she said. 'I had the same print in Cambridge. I wish I'd met your wife.'

'I wish you had too.'

'We Jews understand from experience how the Islamists work. They would rather murder others than deny their own falsehoods. That is why you are so important to this mission.'

'I don't understand.'

'You're a history teacher. Teachers of history are seekers of truth. We are resisting the Islamification of Europe. There is no more noble cause.'

'But they know about the mission, they know everything.'

'We either submit to their tyranny or we resist. Do you not want to play your part, Winston?'

He remembered O'Connell using those same words to him in a Sydney park a long time ago and here he was in an abandoned London church face to face with the leader of the European Resistance. He couldn't go back and he couldn't go forward. He said, 'I agreed to betray you.'

'You had no choice. I understand what extreme pain does.' She held up her crippled hand. She was not an attractive woman by any means but he felt a sudden attraction for her. An image entered his head of making love to her on the worn pew: yes, he could imagine it vividly, seated inside this old stone church with its elegant simplicity. He'd never experienced sexual feelings towards an older woman before. She would be at least sixty. She moved over to his pew and he smelled her faint perfume, felt the heat of her body, saw the soft pale hairs on her cheeks. She was smiling slightly, fingering the glass beads of her necklace. 'You and I are going to kill the Grand Mufti.'

'How?' he said. 'Why me?'

'Together we are going to make history. You will be remembered by those who come after you.'

He stared into her grey eyes, conscious of his own intellectual inferiority. He said, 'I've never killed anyone before.'

Her foot pressed against his. 'Killing is easy, once you know how.'

Unlike Shakespeare, he was riddled with doubts and fears. Despite all that had happened to him he was terribly afraid of dying.

'You have three choices with death, Winston. You can accept it, you can embrace it or you can fear it.'

'I fear it,' he said.

'What is it you fear most?'

'The idea that I won't exist, that tomorrow and the day after people will be going about their lives without me.'

'Where were you before you entered this world? Nowhere. Where will you be after you have departed this world? Nowhere. There is only this one short existence. There is nothing else.'

'That's what frightens me,' he said.

'What a difference it would make if everyone understood this simple truth. The Islamists sacrifice their lives for an idea, but we sacrifice our lives for each other.' She spoke softly, her crippled hand reaching towards his and from the slight tremble of her mouth he understood that she was trying to convince herself as much as convince him. Whatever illness she had contracted from spending her days and nights moving between the dank underground tunnels of London and this small abandoned church it was clear that she was seriously unwell. She coughed again, her body racked with the strain, clasping a handkerchief over her mouth, careful not to spray droplets in the air.

Instinctively he leaned away from her. He looked up at the light pouring in through the cracks and pellet holes in the windows and admired the craftsmanship of this old stone and timber church.

'We lost our way, Winston. We lost confidence in ourselves and in our beliefs. Technology led us into the darkness and separated us from God.'

'So, you believe in God?' He caught the surprise in his own voice.

'Not the vengeful God you are accustomed to hearing of, not Yahweh or Allah, but I believe in something, yes. All living creatures are connected. They are part of us and we are part of them.'

'You mean on a cellular level?'

'God is within us. Not without. What killed the West was the disappearance of its spirituality. We lost our connection to the natural world.'

He wanted to tell her about the passages Sadiq had copied from Avril Blair's notebook: the descriptions of this resourceful English woman planting fruit trees and bulbs, sowing beans, rising early each day to gather eggs, listening to the cries of rooks and gulls, watching a sea eagle ride the air currents while her big brother wracked with TB lay on his bed upstairs in their remote Scottish farmhouse, struggling with the last revisions to his book, begging his friends to send him a refill for his biro. How difficult it was a hundred years ago to buy a biro and yet today you could not find a biro in all of London.

Sadiq had toyed with him, playing the all-knowing, all controlling demiurge for no other reason than to demonstrate that ordinary people like Winston lacked free will, and that the Intelligence Services could determine their actions and emotions whenever they wished. What an idiot he must've appeared. And yet the more he thought about what they'd done to him, the more resolved he was to prove them wrong, to show that he was capable of choosing his own destiny.

Shakespeare smiled as if she could read his thoughts and he looked up at the tall bee-hived bodyguard standing in the aisle behind her. The bodyguard laid a bunch of grapes and a cup of water between them on the pew, and said something that ended in 'Man'.

'Eat,' she said, 'and then we can talk.'

He couldn't recall when he'd last eaten. The pain in his neck made swallowing difficult but the icy cold water soothed his throat. The bodyguard went through the oak door with the carved tympanum and he saw the three women of varying ages arguing among themselves. The door closed and he picked at the sweet black grapes; rather than spit out the seeds he crunched them between his teeth. He wasn't sure if he'd been thinking aloud for Shakespeare was watching him closely.

He said, 'Are there no men on the Council of 12?'

'All our strong men have been silenced or incarcerated,' she said. 'Why did our leaders lie to us? Ask yourself that question.'

'I don't know,' he said. His thoughts were drifting about like balloons. She touched the back of his hand, trying to anchor his attention.

'Our leaders lied to us because they could not admit the enormity of the problem they had created. No-one dared speak the truth. Here in Britain we had tens of thousands of people living in our midst who would murder us for their beliefs. So our leaders deceived us. Soon we lost control of large swathes of our cities. As the attacks grew in Europe they asked what could be the cause of this violence as if it were a mystery.

Yet the ordinary people knew. Thirty years ago, they experienced Paris and Saint-Denis and Stockholm and San Bernardino and Brussels and Boston and Berlin and Barcelona and Hamburg and London and Manchester and Nice and Orlando. They had access to the truth. Even if they didn't know all the details, their instincts told them that this was not merely the work of a few rotten apples.'

'But surely the government knew what was going on?' he said.

'Our political leaders were convinced that if they repeated their lies often enough then eventually the public might come to believe them. We not only tolerated intolerance, but we indulged it,' Shakespeare said. 'For years the so-called experts laughed at the IPGB. No one thought they had a chance. Here was a political party whose stated aim was to impose religious law in England and Wales, to end civil liberties, to curtail freedom of speech. And yet—despite everyone knowing this fact—they won the election! A majority of people in Britain voted for them.

'Twenty-five years ago, I attended a gay pride march in Hyde Park and beside me in the crowd two academic friends of mine were marching arm-in-arm carrying signs. One sign said 'Allah is Gay', the other said 'Jesus is Gay'. Ten minutes into our march, police swarmed on my Malaysian friend with the 'Allah is Gay' sign, confiscated her placard and threatened to arrest her for hate-speech. My other friend with the Jesus sign they ignored. And that, my dear Winston, was the day I realised that our senior police preferred to give a minority privileged status.

'It was the left's blind embrace of the Islamists that allowed them to take power in Britain, and that is what I find so heart-breaking because my whole life I was of the left. With the collapse of ISIS and defeat of the *Khilafa*, the Islamists changed tactics. They foresaw that the easier path to power in the West was not through armed struggle, but through *dawa*, through the great replacement, a high birth-rate combined with mass migration from the war zones. Sleeper cells penetrated every major European capital. This was an invasion by stealth.

'Think of a pack of wild dogs bringing down a wildebeest,' Shakespeare said, 'the wildebeest is much bigger and stronger than the dogs but they pursue her in a pack, they nip at her heels, they snap at her tail, they bite at her nose and gnaw at her flanks until finally, exhausted, she falls and they swarm all over her. That is what has happened in Europe. The Islamists eroded our spirit through their bomb attacks, the shootings, the stabbings, the truck rammings. They used fear and intimidation and victimhood to subjugate us. In their perverted thinking the victims were not the ordinary people maimed and killed by the terror attacks but those Islamists who claim to have been harassed afterwards. They fomented a relentless mix of resentment, deceit and anger. Whenever they couldn't get their way their young men protested by hurling rocks and torching cars until the authorities accommodated their demands for special treatment. We introduced laws to shield them from criticism. But whatever we did was not enough. There will continue to be small pockets of resistance, but the Islamification of Europe is inevitable.'

'That's what Sadiq said.'

'So you've met our Director of Intelligence? We were at Cambridge together. A charming fellow, highly intelligent. And ruthlessly ambitious.'

For Winston, the moment of sexual attraction had passed but he was still gripped by the intensity of this older woman's commitment.

'They're pulling down statues across Britain, removing monuments and inscriptions, altering the names of streets and parks. They are intent on erasing our culture as swiftly as they can. That's why we have chosen you. A teacher of history. Did you know that George Orwell wanted to call his *Nineteen Eighty-Four, The Last Man in Europe*?'

'Yes, Sadiq told me.'

'And did Sadiq tell you where Orwell got the idea? *Der letzte Mensch*—Nietzche's 'Last Man' exists without purpose or direction. There is no longer any distinction between strength and weakness, no innovation or creativity. There is only mediocrity. Individuality and thinking are suppressed. This is the goal our civilization has set for itself under the Islamists. Everyone is the same; whoever thinks otherwise goes to the madhouse.'

Her voice had grown steely. She touched his arm again and he felt a jolt of energy. 'The most effective way to destroy a culture is to destroy its history. This is how Europe will end,' she said. 'Not with a bang but with a whimper.'

Shakespeare stood up and walked to the front of the church and stared up through the lancet windows. A rat scurried along the edge of the wall and vanished between a gap in the stonework. All he made of it was a ball of fur and long black tail and then everything went quiet apart from the buzz of drones flying over the high rises. Coughing, Shakespeare turned and spat into her handkerchief. He saw the streaks of blood. 'Tell me,' she said. 'What have you learned from history?'

'That whatever is true today, may not be true tomorrow.'

She looked at him. 'I like that.'

'Can I ask you a question,' he said. 'What is your real name?'

'Miryam,' she said.

'I think I prefer Shakespeare.'

She wiped her thick-rimmed glasses on her sleeve. The north door opened and the tall Jamaican bodyguard approached. His thick ropy hair twisted on top of his head gave him an extra half-metre in height. He bent and whispered in her ear.

Shakespeare said something in return that Winston couldn't hear. Dwarfed beside her large dark-skinned bodyguard, she could have been any little old lady from London. Instead, she was the Head of the European Resistance, a former activist and Renaissance scholar. So much of her background was clouded in rumour and hearsay, and yet he trusted her. She was different from Sadiq. She understood him.

'Are you ready to play your part, Winston?'

He sat up straight. 'Yes,' he said.

'Good. The most difficult question we face is our own mortality, it takes great courage to accept what awaits us in the end.'

'What is it you want me to do?'

'Take me to them.'

'They'll kill you,' he said. 'They'll execute you like they did Sol Hachuel.'

'Did you not agree to betray me?'

'I had no choice.'

'Now you have a choice.' She smiled. 'Is there anything I can get you?'

'Maybe a notebook and biro.'

'I haven't seen a biro in years.'

The Jamaican bodyguard gave him a knowing—or was it a warning—wink and escorted Shakespeare through the north door. Winston remained alone in the church listening to the pitter-patter of rats beneath the floorboards. He had never been inside a church before. In Australia, no-one attended church anymore. Not for years. It was quiet and warm in here and despite the rats he did not want to leave. His legs still ached and his hands were shaky.

He stared at the afternoon light slanting through the coloured glass. If Shakespeare thought they could get close enough to murder the Grand Mufti she was mistaken. Sadiq was expecting them both. Within minutes of their arrival she'd be cuffed and dragged away to 80 The Strand, London, where she'd be subjected to interrogation; she would confess to every crime imaginable, and be stripped of her dignity. Dishevelled, she'd be paraded before the courts and sentenced to life imprisonment. That's if she was lucky.

The door opened and three women, the ones he had seen earlier in the cavern, came through full of smiles and friendliness. All three wore the drab cotton uniforms of office cleaners or hospital workers, and smelled faintly of soap. They introduced themselves as Claudia, Victoire and Oriana: the youngest was of German origin and was heavily pregnant; Victoire, the middle one, was French and wore a headscarf and blinked a lot; and the eldest one who seemed in charge was short and Italian with black eyes and stood beside the defaced statue of the Virgin Mary, checking her military-style watch.

The middle one sat beside him on the pew and offered him a paper napkin containing figs and strawberries and a sliver of soft cheese. The youngest one sat on his other side cradling her belly and handed him a spiral notebook and pencil stub. 'You like to write things down?' she said and touched his arm. He had never known such attention from strangers. He ate the figs and overripe strawberries while the women told him about the deteriorating situation in their own countries. The middle one's English was limited and it was only through her trembling voice and the grip on his arm that he understood how bad things were in many parts of France. The youngest one told him about her home city in Germany, the assaults, the intimidation. 'We can no longer rely solely on our men,' she said.

When he stood up to stretch his legs, the eldest one, Oriana, asked where he was going. 'Nowhere,' he said. 'Why?'

'Stay here.'

It was not a request. A pistol protruded from the pocket of her pants and he realised these three women were his minders. He sat down, wiped his fingers on his jacket and opened the notebook which was filled with rows of legal costings and found a single blank page. 'What are you writing,' Claudia, the youngest, said.

'I don't know yet.'

'Want to feel my baby?'

He put a hand on her belly and felt a large soft lump shifting about in there.

'It's a girl,' she said.

Claudia was no more than a girl herself, a year or two older than Chelsea with olive skin and dark watchful eyes. She told him that her mother was German and her father was an Indian from Mumbai. 'I worry what sort of Europe my daughter will have to live in,' she said.

'Is there a father?' he said.

'He's in jail in Leipzig. For distributing anti-government leaflets.' The two older women nodded as if they had been entrusted with her safety and the safety of her unborn child. Claudia said, 'Tell him, Oriana, what happened to you.'

Oriana picked up a jagged piece of corner stone that had been dislodged from the church wall and weighed it in her hand.

'Oriana survived the Métro bombing,' said Claudia. 'Go on, tell him.'

'Tell me,' Winston said.

'I was in the middle carriage,' the eldest one said quietly, 'when the bomb went off at the front of the train. The concussion of the blast blew out all the windows and bent the doors. I was ejected through the air and propelled along the aisle. There is really no way to describe what goes through your mind when you think you are going to die. No flash of light. It was so immediate. I became aware of this old woman lying underneath me pleading for help. Her legs were blown off at the knee. I held her hand. There was nothing I could do. The only thing I thought of was that if I survive I will kill the bastards who did this.' She skimmed the broken stone along a pew at the far wall. A rat, startled, raced along the edge of the floorboards so fast it was a blur.

'We've all suffered,' Claudia said. 'Victoire lost her brother and his three-year-old son in Belgium. Mowed down in the Grote Markt.'

Victoire blinked and fiddled with the beads around her neck.

Claudia reminded him of Chelsea the way she liked to talk. Maybe it was her dark hair or maybe it was because so many young women now in London all looked the same but he realised how much he missed Chelsea. He missed her scratchy old records, her rebellious spirit, her sexual energy.

'What about you?' the youngest one said, clutching her belly.

Winston told them about his wife and daughter. He told them how he watched the triple attacks over and over, the same terrifying images broadcast a thousand times. He told them that since their death everyday felt the same. He told them how he had vowed revenge. 'You think you have everything mapped out for your future,' he said, 'and then some fanatic on the other side of the world destroys everyone you loved and everyone you'll ever love.'

The north door opened and the Jamaican came through. His coiled hair brushed against the timber beams of the church. Behind him trailed a woman concealed by a full-length niqab, the flap falling over her eyes.

'Are you ready, Winston?' she said.

'For what?'

'To be fitted.'

He didn't understand what she meant although the three women seemed to know. This mission, he suspected, was doomed. The IIS remained one step ahead; the threat level had been raised to critical. Surely, he would be of more use to the Resistance staying here, he could work in their propaganda unit. He liked writing things down. Winston stared up at the ransacked belfry: in his former life, he'd enjoyed renovating an old decrepit Sydney terrace. If the Resistance agreed he'd be willing to repair the damaged floorboards, seal the cracks, reglaze the church windows, get rid of the rats.

The three women were waiting for his response.

Shakespeare touched his arm: 'It's your choice. You have to make this decision of your own free will.'

It was disturbing to hear her upper-class English voice coming from underneath that niqab. And yet Shakespeare's face was too well known for her to risk walking the streets of London undisguised. If the mob recognised her, they would tear her to pieces. He lowered his head in his hands thinking of what Sarah would have him do. She always said that he would do something to make her proud; she'd believed in him, you only need one good woman to believe in you, and it can change your life.

'So what's your answer, Winston?'

'I'll do it,' he said, though he wasn't exactly sure what she wanted him to do.

The three women embraced him as if they were family. The youngest one, Claudia, kissed his lips. She had beautiful white teeth. 'Your wife and daughter would be proud,' she said. Blinking, Victoire spoke rapidly in French: her words were impassioned and heartfelt and, although he didn't understand much of what she said, it sounded flattering. 'Soon the people of Europe will wake from this nightmare,' the eldest one said, patting her pistol.

Shakespeare lifted the flap of her niqab. 'Take off your jacket.'

He removed his old bomber jacket and stood before the four women and the bodyguard in his jeans and blood-stained tee shirt. Whatever they required of him he was willing to do.

The north door opened. It was Marlon and behind him the bald man they called The Greek with the rimless glasses. Shakespeare said, 'You know Marlon, your handler? He tried to warn you about that young woman—'

'Chelsea? You knew about Chelsea?'

Marlon gave a slow nod of his head. He said, 'We suspected she was being used as bait.'

Surely if they knew Chelsea was living in Sadiq's cellar they should have warned him. Unless it suited their purposes for him to be arrested?

Was that part of their plan? 'So why did you let me go ahead?'

'We didn't *let* you do anything, Winston,' Shakespeare said. 'You made your own decisions.'

'But you could have warned me.'

'Warned you what? Warned you to be careful? We don't control your actions. It was you who begged us to let you spend the night with that young woman.'

'I wasn't in charge of all the information,' he said. The three women were watching him as if this was a morality play. The middle one was twisting a silver heart bracelet on her wrist. The eldest, Oriana, kept checking her watch as if late for an appointment. She said, 'Wake up and smell the Jihad.'

He stared into Shakespeare's face framed by her black niqab. Perhaps she wasn't his friend after all. Or was it simply the clothes she wore that now darkened his view.

'Would you have listened to us if we had told you?' she asked. 'Would you have acted any differently?'

Of course he would. If he had known what they knew he wouldn't have stayed the night, he would have slipped away in the still hours before dawn, before the IIS arrived with their boots and truncheons, before the beatings began, taking Chelsea with him, fleeing London for a remote part of Scotland and somehow they would have survived off the land, digging a vegetable garden, picking wild blackberries, making jam, fetching milk and eggs, skinning rabbits, plucking geese and hens, learning how to live in harmony with the cycles of the earth, and at nights they would both lie exhausted on his bunk, and write up in his notebook all the names of the living creatures they saw: the fishes from the sea, the winged birds in the sky, the seed-bearing plants and fruit-bearing trees, the wildflowers and the nocturnal animals that raided their crops, and despite the many hardships they would have tried to carve out some kind of modest existence together.

That's what he would have done.

The three women were staring at him as if he'd uttered his thoughts aloud. The youngest one, Claudia, rubbed at her belly. The eldest one nodded as if giving a signal. At that moment, The Greek approached from behind Marlon and said, 'Hold your arms out.'

Winston did so.

Gently, he threaded one arm and then the second arm through the openings of a thick padded vest. He pulled the vest up over Winston's shoulders and fastened a strap at the back of his neck and another much larger leather strap around his lower torso. The vest was surprisingly heavy and he could feel the sharp metal objects packed into its canvas pockets and the steel cylinders sewn into the inner lining.

'This red button is the trigger,' the Greek said. 'It's in your right pocket. Be careful where you walk. Don't bump into anyone or anything until you get to the barrier.'

'What's your name?'

'No names,' the Greek said. He helped him back into his jacket, struggling to zip it up.

Winston breathed in deeply and looked around the small church interior at the three women of varying ages, at Marlon and The Greek, at Shakespeare and her bodyguard, their eyes regarding him with respect, if not admiration. This was his family now. He walked towards the north door, Shakespeare following close behind.

Now he understood why the Resistance had chosen him. Now he understood everything.

# 12

He moved through Covent Garden, favouring his left leg. The noise was overwhelming: men chanting and waving banners, their index fingers pointed skywards, covered women ululating with delight and calling out, 'Praise be to Allah!' Never before had London experienced a crowd of this magnitude, a dense heaving mass of pilgrims streaming towards Diversity Square. The Islamists had been in power for 365 days. Soon all of Europe would be theirs. What a magnificent time to be alive. To have faith in the knowledge there was only one truth and that everything that has ever happened and will ever happen is already written.

He stopped in a shop doorway and turned to see who was following. He could not spot Shakespeare in the crowd.

A sign in the window of the shabby little shop said 'No Dogs'. Since he'd arrived in London he had not seen a single dog. Dogs had gone the way of the birds. The sign in the window was spotted with fly dirt and the curtains that were once white were faded and yellow. Paint was peeling from the architraves and grafitti was splashed across the steps and stone corbels. Above the window in large green letters it said 'TEA ROOMS'. Exhausted from his journey and the weight of his vest, he tried the handle and pushed on the glass door. The bell gave a cheery little tinkle as he slipped inside. Tables and chairs were set around an odd L-shaped room and on each table place-mats, teacups and saucers were laid out along with teaspoons and a single white teapot. A clock on the wall had stopped at twelve and apart from a thin layer of dust that coated the floral tablecloths and rat pellets scattered across the floor, this quaint little tea-room resembled the place that his grandmother used to visit in Sydney's Queen Victoria Building with its high tea, willow plates and pink macarons.

There was no sign of any service or customers so he sat at a table by the window and rested his feet on the rung of the opposite chair. He took out his notebook careful not to disturb the thick black wires connected to the red button in his pocket. Crowds surged past his window. Such joy on their faces. Such elation. This was the future and it was so much louder than the past: the air horns, the megaphones, the muezzins, the constant chanting and shouting that Allah is greatest! All this was intended to drown out thought, to leave no room for doubt. Belief was everything.

The window of the little tea-shop shook with the vibrations of thousands of trampling feet. On the other side of the street he spotted the Jamaican bodyguard tying up his bootlaces in a doorway. Beside him was a woman with a pair of large black-framed spectacles sitting on top of her niqab. It was HER. There was no sign of Marlon or The Greek, but Oriana, the eldest of the three women from the church, was standing outside the tea rooms wearing a dark abaya and hijab. She was keeping watch on him. He gripped the pencil in his fingers and started to write: 'I am the last of my tribe, we were destroyed, or more accurately we destroyed ourselves ...'

The door to the tea-rooms flew open, snapping the little silver bell off its chain. The bell rolled across the floor. Oriana gestured from the doorway. Her English was not clear but he understood. He tried to stand, but the weight of the vest filled with screws, nuts, bolts, and sawn lengths of metallic piping pulled on his neck and cramped the muscles in the backs of his legs. He told her he needed to rest a while longer. An enormous volume of noise erupted from half a mile away followed by a roar of cheering. The speeches had begun. If there was one thing the Party excelled at, it was making lengthy speeches.

On the wallscreen Prime Minister Nawaz was preparing the believers for the arrival of the Grand Mufti. Winston watched the crowds streaming west towards the square, tens of thousands of brothers and sisters coming together as a sign of victory. The future had arrived and it was everything the Party had prayed for. He had always known he would do something of consequence, that he would be remembered by those who came after him, that others would take his name just as he had taken his name from a book he had read when he was a boy.

Oriana came inside and clicked the door shut. She stood underneath the floral wall clock that said, 'It's always tea time'. She pulled a pistol from underneath her abaya and waved it towards the stairs. 'What's up there?' she said.

He hadn't thought to look. Although the door to the tea-rooms was unlocked he had assumed the proprietor, along with everyone else, was attending the celebrations. Oriana took the stairs holding her pistol out in front of her and came down moments later with an old couple, bent over and blinking into the light. The old man who must've been ninety at least had a few tufts of hair left on his head and long white eyebrows protruding like an insect's feelers; the woman was as thin and dry as a stick of cinnamon. They stood clasping each other's arm as if they were about to topple face forward. 'You're not going to rob us, daughter, are you?' the old woman said.

Oriana reassured them she was not. She tucked the pistol away under the folds of her abaya and checked her watch.

'We've been robbed three times this year,' the old woman confided. 'My husband forgets to lock the door.'

'I distinctly remember locking it, dear.'

'We were having a nice lie down. We don't get many customers now. Forty five years we've owned this business. We used to get all the fine ladies and gentlemen coming in here. We even had a viscount once, didn't we, Harold?'

The old man nodded, trying to recall.

'People from all over. Americans too. We got a lot of Americans coming through, didn't we, Harold?'

'Yes, dear,' the old man said, trying to recall.

'We always had a good reputation. Ask anyone and they'll tell you Mrs Cranny serves a nice afternoon tea, reasonably priced—'

The door banged open and, ducking his head, the tall Jamaican bodyguard burst through supporting Shakespeare under his arm. He steered her over towards Winston's table and lowered her into a seat by the window, where she started to cough, lightly at first, then removing her glasses, more vigorously until the paroxysm passed. The old couple stared as she struggled to lift the flap of her hijab.

'I told you that latch was broken,' the old man said. 'We need to ring somebody.'

'I would die for a nice cup of tea,' Shakespeare said. 'Me too,' said her bodyguard and Oriana, preoccupied with the mechanisms of her watch, nodded in agreement.

'What about you, Winston?'

'I would love a cup and something to eat if possible.'

All the colour returned to the old woman's face as if he had paid her a compliment. This old English couple reminded him of a pair of hedgehogs, prickly-haired, shrivelled-up from a lifetime of work and partly blind. 'I'll put the kettle on then,' the old woman said, and, gripping her husband's arm, they shuffled out to the kitchen.

'Time for you, and time for me,' Shakespeare said. 'After the cups, the marmalade, the tea—'

'What's that?' Winston asked.

'Something I used to teach.' Her face framed by the black niqab resembled an early Renaissance portrait: the long nose, the thought-riddled forehead, lips firmly set together, but it was her steely gaze behind those over-sized glasses that fixed his attention. Despite her infirmity she carried an aura of defiance.

He snapped his notebook shut and said, 'Do you ever regret speaking out?'

'I only wish I had spoken out more,' Shakespeare said.

'Where are the others?'

The others, she informed him, were back at the church. He understood this to mean Marlon and the one they called The Greek and Victoire and the pregnant girl, who was due in a few weeks. 'Claudia wants to give birth in the church,' Oriana said. The muscled Jamaican bodyguard and Oriana were seated at the adjacent table and every time he reached out to touch her hand she pulled it away.

The tea arrived. The old man pushing a wobbly trolley and his wife clattering plates and spoons. A fly lay upside down on the edge of his saucer and Winston flicked it onto the floor; the tablecloth was stained brown at the edges, but all he could think of was a cup of tea.

'You might like to try one of my rock cakes.' The old woman passed him a biscuit with her tongs. When he dunked it in his tea it softened and tasted sweeter than expected. 'Very nice,' he said. The old woman's wrinkled face lit with pleasure as if serving tea was the most rewarding occupation. 'Did you lock the door, Harold?'

'Yes, I did, dear.'

Crowds were streaming past the tea-shop window but not once did this old couple look outside or glance up at the wallscreen. It was as if the old woman and her husband had grown oblivious to the world outside. Winston watched him squeeze his wife's wrist at intervals to reassure her of his presence. What he would give right now to be able to hold Sarah's hand. He remembered making love to her in the Royal

National Park, as shameless as wild animals. What had always attracted him about Sarah was the ease of her company, her naturalness. How insecure the Islamists must be to hide their women, she used to say, there is no dignity in being covered from head to foot.

Watching Shakespeare across the table, with her black gloves clasping her floral cup, he asked himself what Sarah would have thought if she could have seen the leader of the European Resistance right now. He picked a sultana off his plate and sipped at his tea, not wishing to release his grip on the past. Everyone gets one piece of good luck in their life and meeting Sarah was his.

'We must hurry,' Oriana said.

'I haven't finished my tea,' he said.

'There is time,' Shakespeare told her. 'The target hasn't arrived.'

On the wallscreen a famous author was praising the Party's virtues, its compassion, its humanistic richness. His conversion shortly after the elections had proven advantageous, for his prize-winning memoir was now recommended reading by the Party. A succession of professors stepped up to the podium to speak of the outstanding contribution the IPGB had made to British culture, how their faith was the most extraordinary moral force in the world today.

Winston listened while he drank his tea but the words had no impact. He was thinking of Sarah and Tess and what had happened to them in Atlanta. No matter how much he shifted in his chair he felt uncomfortable, weighed down by his vest. It must have weighed ten kilos at least. The Greek had warned him at the church that the explosive, a mixture of acetone, hydrogen peroxide and hydrochloric acid, was highly sensitive to impact, temperature change and friction. 'You will need to get within one hundred metres of the target,' the Greek said. 'Don't worry, you won't feel a thing. Your brain won't have time to receive the pain signals.' The detonation velocity, he explained, was around 28,000 feet per second, twenty times faster than a 9-mm bullet leaving the muzzle of a hand gun. Death would be *instantaneous.* It was the same word that woman from the Consular Services had consoled him with on the phone call from Atlanta.

Winston raised his head to see the English couple wheeling their old chrome trolley towards them. 'More tea anyone?' the old woman said.

'Not right now,' Shakespeare told her.

'I know who you are,' the old woman whispered. 'Soon as I saw your face I said to Harold that's her, the Jewess. God bless you, for what you're doing—' She gasped. 'Oh, I'm sorry.' She glanced up at the wallscreen.

'Doesn't matter,' Winston said. The IIS knew where they were. All four of them would have been tracked from the minute they left that old broken-down Saxon church. There was nothing he could do to alter the future. He would betray the Jewess and then embrace the Party. Those were his instructions. It was the will of Allah.

Shakespeare finished her tea and wiped her mouth. 'Nothing more civilized than a good cup of tea,' she said. On the wallscreen London's new Metropolitan Police commissioner was speaking of the 740 arrests made in the past week for blasphemy. 'Let us be clear,' he said firmly. 'We will not tolerate any form of insulting or disrespectful speech.' Behind him a line of dignitaries and minor royals were being ushered to their seats.

Shakespeare fixed him with a glassy stare: 'The wars of the future will no longer be *between* nations,' she said. 'They will be *within* nations.' She leaned across the stained tablecloth until he could see the pores of her skin. 'Look out the window,' she said. 'What do you see?'

'I see people celebrating,' he said. 'I see the streets filled with the Party's supporters. I see the future.' He recalled Sadiq's words: 'if you believe in nothing, then nothing is all you are left with'. He was right. It was the Islamists' belief that had emboldened them, that had given them such confidence.

'If a culture is weakened,' Shakespeare said, 'its centre cannot hold. Today is the day, God willing. The good people of England will remember 24 October 2048, just as they remember 5 November 1605. We will make history, you and I.'

He was not afraid. At the last moment he would drop to his knees, unzip his jacket and reveal the jumble of wires taped to his vest. That's what he had planned. He was no hero. They had let him walk from that cell knowing the crimes he had committed, the blasphemy he had uttered, the hatred he had in his heart. Why did Sadiq let him go? How could he be so confident that he would do his bidding?

Cameras panned across Diversity Square showing the faces of pilgrims delirious with joy, boys perched on the shoulders of fathers, uncles and brothers. Who could deny them now? London was theirs. All that was written had come to pass.

The Jamaican bodyguard and Oriana were sitting at the next table, both of them watching the front door as if expecting an intrusion. Oriana had one hand hidden inside her abaya. He admired her fearlessness. She was clearly a trained fighter and her presence here, he suspected, was to ensure he carried out his mission.

He turned his attention to Shakespeare, the one the Islamists felt threatened by, yet to see her in the flesh like this she looked so weak and helpless. The Party feared intelligent women. It suited their purposes to exaggerate the danger from the Resistance and to magnify their numbers. In the cavern he had estimated the Resistance consisted of no more than a few hundred followers including a handful of trained fighters like these two at the next table, Oriana, and the huge Jamaican bodyguard she called Jarvis. The government needed the Resistance to justify the billions of pounds they had spent in a single year on upgrading security and surveillance.

Winston remembered the words Sadiq had uttered to him in that brightly-lit cell: 'Europe needs to be revitalised. It is broken and decadent. Homosexuals kiss in your bars, your women are loose and promiscuous, you produce sad, troubled children. You are a dead culture but we will give you life.'

Perhaps Sadiq was right. That even though people in the West thought they were making their own decisions, those decisions, in fact, were being made for them. There was no escape, no privacy; the Party was all seeing, all hearing, all knowing. You could not hope to defeat them, all you could do was accept and obey and then everything would be all right. That's what Sadiq had promised. All he had to do was obey, and his life and Chelsea's would be spared. He could start anew. It was not impossible. Shakespeare was dying, the Resistance was finished and the Party would rule Britain for a thousand years. Did it really matter what happened to the rest of Europe? Nations suffer the fate they deserve. He had to look after himself, hold onto what life he had left.

'Tell me Winston,' she said, as if she knew what he was thinking. 'What do you believe in?'

'I believe in love.'

'The Islamists love Allah more than their own children. We are fighting ignorance. Yesterday, I heard Prime Minister Nawaz boast that the apostle Paul was born in Turkey. The BBC interviewer agreed this was an astonishing fact, that one of the first Christians was actually Turkish. Nothing was mentioned that Turkey as a nation didn't exist then, that Paul was a Jew. But that is how the Party work—they tell half-truths—they infect the past with their lies and distortions. That is why the role of history is so important. If there is no history you can claim anything, the truth becomes whatever you deem it to be.'

The wallscreen began blaring news of a major anti-terror operation underway in Central London. Security agencies were on high alert. He shut his eyes. How fortunate he was to have loved and been in love. A memory of Sarah came to mind of the night she gave birth to their premature daughter, refusing any pain relief while he marvelled at her determination.

'You can live your life in ignorance,' Sarah used to say, 'or you can open your eyes to what is happening all around you'. She had opened his eyes, made him see the world anew.

'Is it time?' Shakespeare said.

Oriana nodded. The bodyguard removed his hand from her lap. Whatever they had going on was no longer secret. A roar from the crowd erupted outside and there he was on the wallscreen: a large man with a black beard, dressed in the all-white regalia that identified him as the spiritual leader of the Party, riding in a long, armoured limousine through the streets of London. What a majestic sight he made in his white turban and his white jubbah thobe with the wooden buttons open at the front, seated high in the rear of that glass-topped vehicle, waving at the tens of thousands of believers lining the streets and the hundreds of millions watching on their wallscreens.

Slowly the triumphant procession rolled towards the Square where the crowds had massed in even greater numbers. The cameras switched to the Royal Gardens where the old King, his wine-red waistcoat bristling with ribbons and decorations, was giving a welcoming speech.

'I appeal to everyone in Britain to celebrate our strong moral values,' he declared. 'London is now a beacon of tolerance, acceptance and diversity.' The old King spoke of the inner peace and serenity he had found from his recent marriage and cast a glance at his covered young bride standing several feet behind him, tall and slender with wide knowing eyes.

Supported by her bodyguard, Shakespeare rose from the table. Her face was grey and she was barely able to speak. 'Be strong, Winston,' she said. 'Be brave.'

He went through the kitchen and found the proprietor and her husband huddled near the urn. From the agitated look in their eyes, he understood. They had alerted the authorities. He couldn't blame them. What choice did they have? He paid for the tea and cake with his last wrinkled pound notes and left the old couple embracing in a corner, inseparable to the end.

Oriana opened the front door and Shakespeare pulled down the flap of her niqab to conceal her face. 'Give me your arm,' she said to Winston. They stepped outside and the noise of the crowd swallowed them up. Special Islamic Police guarded every corner, four, five, six at a time, armed and alert. It was hot on the street and he sweated under his bomber jacket and vest; sharp metal edges dug into his chest and he struggled to remain upright. He feared his bulky clothing would raise suspicions but the SIPs gave him only a cursory glance as if this sickly old woman clinging to his arm was his grandmother. Somewhere behind them Oriana and the Jamaican bodyguard were battling to keep up.

The flow of people towards the square had its own momentum and they let themselves be carried along with the current, past signs written in Bengali, Punjabi and Pashto. Shakespeare coughed repeatedly under her niqab. She didn't speak and it struck him as strange that the woman his wife had admired most in all of Europe was now completely reliant on him to carry out her wishes. He felt inferior to her intellectually and yet at any moment he could betray her and there was nothing she could do to prevent it. He was in control. For the first time since he'd set foot in London his fate lay in his own hands. He made the decisions, not Sadiq, not the Resistance, not HER.

'I wish we could have spoken more,' she said. 'Got to know each other better.'

It was hard to hear her with all the noise around them and with her sporadic fits of coughing, but as they were swept along by the crowd she told him about Marlon, how he had lost his career and his husband.

'Can I call you Miryam?' It didn't seem right to call her Shakespeare any longer. She was just an ailing old Englishwoman. He put his arm round her shoulders and drew her closer. He sensed she was about to collapse and only his arm was keeping her upright. When he turned he saw Oriana and the Jamaican trying to barge their way forward to reach them. The air smelled of burning kerosene. Down a laneway a group of teenage boys was setting fire to something on the road. Winston assumed it was a flag.

A hand grabbed his shoulder and the Jamaican bodyguard lifted the weight of Shakespeare from his arm. What a relief to let her go. Oriana pressed against his other side. 'How is she?'

'She can't go much further.'

People closed in around them: young men twirling their shirts and chequered scarves, chanting 'Freedom Go to Hell'. Trying to move through the dense crowd was impossible, people throwing petals in the air, with cries of exultation and joy. Winston kept his hands in his pockets while Oriana in front, dragging one foot behind her, tried to shield him from the pushing and shoving. The air smelled of the river and the overburdened sewage lines. They stopped on the road at the far edge of the square.

He looked up at the drones, black specks in the bleached London sky, at the electronic eyes blinking from windows, and the heavily-armed police and soldiers everywhere. A huge banner proclaimed that the Party was 'Keeping Britain Safe'. Even if Winston had wanted to detonate his vest, he was too far away. His finger hovered over the trigger: 'everything from the hands of your watch to the bones of your wrists will become shrapnel,' the Greek had said, 'the level of heat and pressure will melt iron.'

He would wait until the very last moment. It was his decision; his alone. Surely the IIS were tracking their movements, and yet they made no move to arrest her. It surprised him that Sadiq had let Shakespeare get this close. Her coughing had ceased and when he grabbed her deformed hand she squeezed his fingers feebly in reply, the Jamaican supporting her other side. He'd imagined the IIS would have swooped long before Shakespeare reached the square. An image came to mind of Chelsea covering her mouth. 'Just as her teeth were infecting her gums,' Sadiq said, 'so, too, was this young woman infecting men with her filthy-mindedness.'

They shuffled past the towering column. Horatio Nelson was gone and in its place the Party had erected a new sandstone statue. 'To the memory of Olaudah Equiano', the inscription read, 'who fought against slavery.' Whoever he was, Winston had never heard of him.

And there in the distance was the Grand Mufti of London, Haj Amin al-Qaradawi, emerging onto an enormous stage in front of the National Gallery, surrounded by blast-proof steel barriers. He held up the palm of one hand and said into the microphones: 'There is no God but God and Muhammad is his prophet!'

The crowd responded with an enormous roar, so loud it drowned out the sound of the jets overhead.

The Grand Mufti raised his hand again. 'In one year we have made great strides in Britain,' he declared. 'We have replaced the institutions of the kuffar with the laws of Allah. Is this not our divine right? Is this not our sacred duty?' A Muslim must obey the Sharia and the Sharia alone! We will conquer Europe, we will conquer America! Not through the sword, but through *dawa*!'

Feverish waves of cheering spilled across the square. It was a spectacle like nothing Winston had ever experienced before: the intensity, the sheer excitement and emotion on people's faces; the smell of so many dusty, sweating bodies pressed together in the sticky heat. If only he had his notebook, if only he could record what he was witnessing: the triumphant Grand Mufti clothed all in white, waving one hand like a baton at the crowd. He spoke of the four major *Khilafahs,* the Rashiduns, the Umayyads, the Abbasids and the Ottomans. He spoke of the great Islamic inventions throughout recorded history. He spoke of how the Sharia should be implemented gradually.

The Grand Mufti waited for the enormous volume of cheering to subside and then he raised his other hand in the air and the crowd went silent.

'From today,' he promised, 'there will be unlimited freedom for everyone in Britain, rich and poor, young and old. This freedom will extend into all aspects of daily life.' He called on the public to report seditionist elements and warned that anyone who insults the sanctities of the Party would be dealt with severely. His delivery was compelling. Who could dismiss the promise of a better life for all Britons regardless of race and ethnicity, regardless of birth and wealth, regardless of how you spoke or where you lived? In a troubled, fractured world, Winston understood that the simplest of answers now had the widest appeal. To belong and to believe was all that mattered.

'Let the festivities begin,' the Grand Mufti declared. The sleeves of his long white clerical robes dangled over his wrists, and he stood in front of the turbulent sea of supporters, bathing in the acclamation.

It was impossible to move. Winston felt Shakespeare's hand grip his elbow. Between the upper edge of her niqab and the flap of the chador, her weary grey eyes stared at him.

'Tell me, Miryam,' he said, 'how long before we die?'

'Not long now. Are you still afraid?'

'Yes,' he said.

'Remember your wife and daughter. You'll be with them shortly.'

'With them where?'

'Wherever the dead go,' she said. 'Once you accept your fate there is no fear.'

She was right. Why was he so afraid of death? He had lived and loved two people more than he had loved himself. Was that not the purpose in life, to love beyond yourself? He thought of Sarah—she loved him, she'd said, and although he doubted it at times, he took her at her word. He knew about her infidelities: the intense friendships with the bright young men she encountered at her rallies and meetings. He could never accept that her liaisons were as insignificant as she claimed, but afterwards she was always honest. 'Things just happened,' she said, as if it were beyond her control. 'It was just sex,' she said another time, as if she believed that the casualness of her encounters might console him. He tried not to imagine the woman he loved undressing, kissing and making love to another man in a strange bedroom but the scenarios haunted his thoughts. No matter how rational she sounded, no matter how reasonable and considered, he was never convinced. Many times he wished he'd had the courage to leave her, but he couldn't. He was the rock, the reliable high-school teacher, caring for their baby daughter while Sarah spent hours recruiting and organising, passionate in her support for the cause. He hated to admit it, even to himself, but he was an old-fashioned monogamist.

'Over there.' She looked towards a group of SIPs, armed with semi-automatic weapons, standing two hundred metres away. 'They're watching us.'

He was surprised it had taken this long.

'We need to get him through the barriers,' she told the other two. Oriana drew her pistol from under her abaya. 'Never fear,' Oriana said. 'Killing Jihadis is what I do best.'

Only when the Jamaican pushed through the crowd in the direction of the armed police did Winston realise what was happening. 'There is no paradise!' Oriana cried as the Jamaican shoved pilgrims aside, cutting a path for Oriana to follow. Startled, the SIPs began speaking excitedly into their pocket screens, shifting their attention from Shakespeare to this huge black man with the coiled hair coming straight for them and the short, covered woman behind, waving her pistol recklessly in the air. People dived to get out of their way, drones circled overhead, and the shouts and exultations of so many pilgrims crammed into Diversity Square added to the confusion of what was happening. Winston saw two SIPs back away, weapons raised. The crowd around them was unaware of what was going down, the noises and roar from the Party's loudspeakers and the lavish military display overhead disordering their senses.

How brave Oriana was. 'If we don't fight them today,' she'd whispered in the church, 'we shall be their whores tomorrow.'

A shot rang out and then another, two loud cracks like a branch snapping. The Jamaican, the one called Jarvis, threw up an arm to the side of his head as if to bat away an insect and bright red blood spilled from the entry wound above his ear; he toppled forward into the crowd as if he had been felled with an axe. Only then did the screaming start, people pushing and shoving one another, trapped with nowhere to go. In the distance, the Grand Mufti was being hustled off stage and police began moving through the crowd.

'Is the moment come?' Winston said.

'Yes.'

He couldn't see if Oriana was down, but the SIPs with weapons drawn were standing in a tight circle staring at something lying on the ground.

Shakespeare lifted the flap of her chador, making sure that the men around her could see her face. She kissed his lips and said: 'What you are about to do, do quickly. Go now and don't look back.'

He smelt the sourness of her breath before she yanked the niqab off over her head and stood exposed in the middle of the crowd. This woman who had led the Resistance and been the hope of so many people in Europe, standing there in the London sunshine in her dark bra and underpants, with her wrinkled skin, holding her head up defiantly, daring to be recognized.

'Put your clothes on, grandma!' someone said.

Another man cried: 'It's the Jewess!'

Men closed in around her, young men dressed in western clothes. One of them struck her face with his fist.

She didn't call out, she stood before them, her nose bloodied, as they lashed out, punching and striking.

'Beat her! Beat her!' they urged.

One man dislodged a paving stone from the road and bounced it off her temple, another man struck her repeatedly with the heel of his sandal. Older men leaned across holding up their pocket screens to record the punishment.

'A British Jewess I was born!' she yelled, 'and a British Jewess I will die!'

Her defiance only increased the attacks. 'Keep her upright!' they cried. 'Don't let her fall.' More men joined in the assault. This she-devil was working for the Americans. She was evil. 'Damn you!' they cried. Smashing her face with their fists, kicking her as she slid to her knees, pelting her with anything they could prise off the road or wrench from the monuments.

Winston turned away quickly and began to walk through the thinned-out crowd towards the police lines. A roar erupted behind him as loud as if England had scored a last-minute goal against Germany.

'The Jewess has been killed! The Jewess has been killed!'

Winston stared into the joyful faces he passed. The terrorists had been defeated! The Party had triumphed! Strangers smiled at him and he smiled back in accord. 'Peace be with you. Inshallah!'

What was the point of carrying out the attack now? Shakespeare was dead. Had he not carried out Sadiq's orders? Had he not brought them the Jewess? 'Let me through,' he cried, 'let me through here!'

The barrier was ringed with militarized police in full riot gear. Eyes were all he could see behind the balaclavas, shields and visors. What had he expected by coming to London: he had expected betrayal; he had expected death. He felt the trigger in his pocket. If only he had Shakespeare's courage, if only he didn't cling so stubbornly to life. There was no fantasy world waiting for him to enter.

'Let me pass,' he said. The wall of riot police stared back with an intimidating silence: he was not getting through; any moment they would advance with helmets, clubs and mace. A giant electronic sign flashed above the columns of the gallery: 'Keeping Britain Safe'. The Grand Mufti was nowhere to be seen but his voice boomed from hidden screens denouncing the enemies of the Party.

One of the black-clad police drew an e-device from his duty belt and barked at him to place both hands in the air. They were going to search him. In a panic, Winston blurted, 'I'm working for the IIS.' He realised he didn't know Sadiq's surname. He squinted, thumb touching the trigger, feeling the weight of the explosives, the metal and wire strapped to his chest, mustering all his courage. 'Sadiq!' he cried out. 'I'm working for Sadiq!'

The wall of police parted as if he had uttered a magical phrase and he slipped through the checkpoint and past the armoured MRVs. Standing in front of a row of concrete barriers, Sadiq was talking to a group of senior Party members. They stared at him for a long moment as if he were an alien.

'Well done, Mr Smith,' Sadiq said. 'I knew you would not disappoint. You will be rewarded for your loyalty.'

The casualness of his greeting disturbed Winston, as if Sadiq was an old friend rather than the man responsible for his recent torture. He wore a dark suit, open-necked white shirt, and a self-satisfied smile that said I am more intelligent than you can imagine.

'His Eminence wants to thank you in person.'

'Really?' Winston said.

Sadiq waved him through the barriers daubed in green and black Party slogans. Beyond these giant blocks a second ring of blast-proof steel plates prevented vehicular access to the forecourt of the National Gallery. Everywhere there were soldiers and specialised police units with semi-automatic weapons and yet he had made it this far without being searched. Why hadn't Sadiq ordered his men to remove his vest? He glanced behind him but Sadiq was gone and so too were the men he had been speaking with. Why would the IIS allow him to enter a restricted area when they knew he was wired?

And then he realized: how naive he was, how incredibly stupid! Sadiq had never intended letting him go. He wanted the attack to proceed. So what if a handful of police officers and Party functionaries were killed? He had served his purpose by bringing them the Jewess and now they had one last use for him. All along this was their aim, a terror attack in a crowded public square on the anniversary of the Party's electoral victory. The outrage that would ensue, the outpouring of grief and sympathy the government would receive world-wide. The dead would be acknowledged as martyrs, admitted to Jannah and their families recompensed. This was why he had not been searched, why he had sailed through that checkpoint so easily. The IPGB wanted him to carry out his mission in order to tighten their control, to justify their crackdown on what could be said or thought in Britain. They needed the Resistance to exist; otherwise from whom were they keeping Britain safe?

It all made sense now. From the moment he had stepped off that plane they had steered him like a goat. You think you are determining your own life, you think you are master of your own fate, when you are no more than a leaf in a storm. Sadiq was right: free will was a myth.

Snipers were positioned at the windows and along the upper ledges of the Gallery. They patrolled the rooftops of adjoining buildings and crouched in their modified MRVs parked on the terraces. If he threw up his hands now and exposed his vest they would shoot him without hesitation. They could not afford to let him live. It made no difference if the attack was foiled. Whatever he did he was still carrying out their wishes. Only the Party was capable of protecting the people. The crowds had dispersed towards The Mall and Whitehall, where food trucks were dispensing barrels of rice and chicken, and fresh fruit and sweets. The generosity of the Party knew no bounds.

Winston stepped between the blast-proof barriers and inside the perimeter where only senior Party members in their distinctive dark suits and white shirts unbuttoned at the neck were permitted. The Grand Mufti was standing beneath a black and white flag at the entrance to the gallery seemingly unaware of what was happening. There were police everywhere, specialized army units and militia with their fingers curled around the triggers of their weapons, running their eyes over him as if they could read his mind.

Slowly he approached the foot of the steps, his heart racing, taking deep breaths. Armed police spilled across the square. What had happened to Oriana he didn't know. Any minute now he expected a bullet to enter his brain. His vest was filled with explosives connected by a wire to the trigger in his pocket. Such a simple, cheap and effective device. He remembered Sadiq words: 'Your only choice is what we allow you to choose.' He was within a hundred metres of them now, close enough for them to experience the full force of the blast.

If he could write down his thoughts, he would write that all his life had been leading up to this moment: this incredible sense of power. There was nothing like it. These people around me don't realize their lives rest in my hands. I don't belong here anymore among the living. I'm tired of all the noise, the crowds. I'm tired of London. But where I am going is not to a better place, it's not even a place. Hard to believe that in a few short seconds I will not exist and the world will continue on without me. No virgins await, no sweet-smelling houris, only nothingness. Strange not to go on wishing one's wishes, thinking one's thoughts, no need for breathing; no need for anything. There will be no white light, no time for my pain receptors to send their messages to my brain, only the extreme heat of the blast as my organs—liver, spleen, heart, bowel and lungs—are torn from my flesh, my limbs dismembered, my head flung through the air, and my eyeballs liquified. How do you come to terms with such an end? Do you seek refuge in some childish afterlife? Or do you have the courage to face the truth?

Winston unzipped his bomber jacket with his left hand to reveal the vest with the red wire sticking out and saw a flicker of panic in the eyes of the Grand Mufti and his followers standing between the columns in their flowing white robes. Thickset bodyguards fumbled for their pistols, and in that fraction of a second he recalled Sadiq's words in the prison cell: 'You kuffars believe in nothing.'

But Sadiq was wrong. He did believe in something. Something more important than an imaginary God. He gripped the trigger, thumb pressing down. This was his decision, his alone. He had never felt so alive. He looked up at the London sunshine, the light shining through the gloom. A memory of Sarah came to mind. Despite her betrayals he loved her deeply. He was no longer afraid of death. He understood now that he was doing this for love. All that mattered was love. Love was everything.

# ABOUT THE AUTHOR

John Dale is the author of seven books including the campus novel *Leaving Suzie Pye*, which was translated into Turkish, and a novella *Plenty*. His best-selling true-crime biography *Huckstepp* was the winner of a Ned Kelly award, as was the first of his three crime novels. He has also published *Wild Life*, a memoir of his grandfather, and edited three anthologies, including the recent *Sydney Noir*. He is a Professor of Writing at UTS.

www.ingramcontent.com/pod-product-compliance
Ingram Content Group Australia Pty Ltd
76 Discovery Rd, Dandenong South VIC 3175, AU
AUHW020136130726
429791AU00003B/104

9 781925 801729